Saigon Dreaming

SAIGON DREAMING

Recollections of Indochina Days

Tela Zasloff

ST. MARTIN'S PRESS / NEW YORK

Excerpts from *Saigon Dreaming* first appeared in *Granta* 26, "Travel Writing," published in spring 1989.

© Tela Zasloff 1990

First published in the United States of America in 1990

Printed in the United States of America

ISBN 0-312-04216-7

Design by Amelia R. Mayone

Library of Congress Cataloging-in-Publication Data

Zasloff, Tela.
      Saigon dreaming: recollections of Indochina days/Tela Zasloff.
           p.   cm.
      ISBN 0-312-04216-7
        1. Indochina—Description and travel. 2. Zasloff, Tela—
Journeys—Indochina.   I. Title.
    DS535.Z37   1990
    915.9704—dc20   90-30001
                                                   CIP

To Joe

CONTENTS

Saigon Dreaming

When I was twenty-five, I married and went to Saigon. That new home was a decaying city, the center of an accelerating war that America was supporting but barely understood. In fact, to understand the war was the reason Joe took me there—to conduct a political study of the Vietnamese Communists. The conclusions of the study would be prescient about the course of the war, and earned the respect and attention of high officials in the U.S. government.

But Saigon was not really a city at war for me, neither at the time nor now when I think back across twenty-five years. Saigon was a disturbing dream, like the ones we have immediately before waking in the morning, a confusion of vague but pressing responsibilities, people making strange demands, and tense muscles frozen in action.

In 1964 somnolence was still possible. The actual war was out there in the countryside. We could sense it only by the increase of uniformed men in the streets and occasional sounds of artillery, although these were indistinguishable from thunder claps or the sonic booms of airplanes overhead.

At the time I was only dimly aware of the course of events, dazzled by the gracious French provincialism that still overlay the buildings and style of life and by the international sophistication represented at every dinner party. Saigon had long been attractive to foreigners and paid court to them even before the era of French control. In fact the Chinese name for Saigon, which the French adopted, is made up of two characters that express Saigon's historical position toward China—"Western tribute payer."

But it was evident to the experienced resident that Saigon was becoming toxic. The question being asked at the time was what could America do to stem the process of self-destruction in Saigon and prevent a Communist victory. The small number in 1964 who answered "Nothing but get out" were popularly considered either defeatist or betrayers of friends. In February 1965, two months after we left Saigon, President Johnson chose to send the first contingent of American combat forces to Vietnamese soil. In the following ten years of war, over 55,000 Americans were killed.

I had no notion then that 1964 would be a crucial turning point of the Vietnam War for the United States. But I remember vividly that even in the smallest details of our life during those days, there was a smell of decay, sometimes strong like rotting meat, sometimes sweet like flowers too long in a vase.

176 Rue Pasteur

Our house had been elegant, in the provincial French manner, a square, two-story concrete building with balconies across the front second floor and verandas in front and back. The low-built servants' quarters were across the back driveway, which was lined with storm drains that housed rats as big as cats. Vines of bright pink blossoms climbed into our windows and across the tiny plot of grass to the tall, spiked iron gate blocking the front driveway, where we left our garbage cans for collection by the U.S. Military Assistance Command. Like all the houses on the street, ours was surrounded by a ten-foot-high concrete wall, with barbed wire strung across the top to discourage thieves or political zealots. Almost every day, a small, stooping gardener appeared, his face covered by a floppy straw hat. He never spoke, tipped his head slightly in our direction when we came out the front door, and spaded assiduously in our small front yard, apparently weeding and caring for the narrow strip of grass, hanging plants, hibiscus tree, and flowers deposited there by the former residents.

In that summer of 1964, the house belonged to the U.S. military, whose Vietnamese employees cheerfully moved us in— after removing the old bedding by tossing it over the railings of the second-floor balconies. They fixed our toilets and pounded in nails and boards wherever we asked. The inside of the house was spacious and airy, with grillwork and shutters guarding the windows and large ceiling fans whirring until sundown. The ground floor comprised one large space the size of a hotel lobby, divided by a tall bamboo room divider hung with three potted plants that struggled for life in the cool darkness and artificial light. On the ledge of this divider sat one small, comical cactus plant to which I was especially attached. This assembly separated the rattan and flowered furniture of the living room from the dining area.

Besides the kitchen and pantry, announced by the usual ceramic water filter at the pantry entrance, there was only one other room on the ground floor, which became the project office. All the floors were smooth red tile, wet mopped twice a day by Chi Hai, or rather by Chi Bai, working under Chi Hai's impatient and sometimes nasty supervision. The kitchen and pantry belonged to Anh Ba, who cooked, shopped, and directed everything to do with meals, including Chi Hai's service, which he oversaw with continual displeasure.

The stairway to the second floor took one turn and had two long, polished cherry-wood handrails that were smooth and pleasing to run your hand along. On the second floor, all the front rooms were used as offices. We tried sitting out on the front balconies in the evening, but the blue smoke from the city's misfiring cars and hordes of small motor scooters drove us indoors to air conditioning. Our bedroom and bath were in the back. The bathtub was a strange affair, long and deep, with wide ledges and sloping sides, carved in one piece out of a smooth rose-colored and black-speckled cement. It was obviously designed for someone tall and narrow-hipped who could slide in like a seal. Below the necessary ceramic filter for drinking water was a built-in toilet paper holder that dispensed small brown sheets as coarse as paper bags.

We could open the black wooden shutters of our bedroom window and look out on the servants' quarters strung with lines of our daily-washed clothes, and across to the high wall and rooftop of our unknown neighbor.

Domestics

Dealing with servants is the most intimate aspect of a foreign stay and the most difficult for American women trying to run their households as they do in the States. The subject dominated women's conversations at dinner parties and threatened to drive out all other topics. Our servants, as professional a crew as any, soon realized that I knew nothing about the profession and tried as gently and considerately as possible to break me in.

Our cook was Anh Ba (not his real name but a designation of his position in his family). He was a sharp-boned, intelligent, severe-looking man with a round, sweet-faced wife and nine children who helped prepare for cocktail parties when we served Vietnamese hors d'oeuvres that required much chopping and wrapping. Ba discussed the accounts with me every few days in his sparse and my halting French, but otherwise he frowned if I walked into the kitchen area or tried to discuss menus.

He preferred putting out French-style meals (he had cooked for a French general before us), which meant a heavy meal at noon, including a meat dish and pastry for dessert. He did not regard preparation of Vietnamese meals as anything special—although we preferred them—and kept on baking his French pastries despite my tentative requests that he serve only fruit for dessert. He finally complied when told that Monsieur was unhappy because he was getting too fat. He gave a rare smile and nodded. Despite warnings from experienced U.S. military wives that cooks always cheat on expenses, after a few weeks of finding that his lists of purchases and figures always added up, I grew tired of being vigilant and decided to trust him. I recorded later that over a five-month period he had spent 37,430 piasters on food and kitchenware (the equivalent of $520 U.S. at the official exchange rate). This did not seem unreasonable.

A crisis occurred over Ba's pay. After three weeks with us, he appeared in the living room one afternoon—where I was reading—cleared his throat, and stiffly asked how much I intended to pay him. He shook his head to my answer of 2,700 piasters a month and said he would talk to Monsieur. On the day that Khanh declared himself President of South Vietnam, Ba and Monsieur settled on a salary of 2,300 piasters for the first month, 2,700 the second, and 3,000 after that, which was high pay at that time. I resented Ba's bargaining and what I considered lack of appreciation of my hands-off attitude toward his cooking, particularly when he remarked—cavalierly, I thought—that to Madame, a few hundred piasters one way or the other made no difference. But then bargaining, whether for wages or purchases, was a cultural dance I could not follow.

My attempted parsimony was also prompted by admonitions from U.S. officials that Americans not drive up the rates of wages and prices in Saigon. This created resentment among the Saigon bourgeoisie and foreign residents whose funds were not so plentiful. Overpaying would also show us to be naïve newcomers who did not understand how things worked. Ba was right, though, that it was difficult for an American to bargain for what amounted to a few dollars difference at a time when taxi fare was about fifteen cents, shoes, a dollar and a quarter, a silk handmade dress, twelve dollars, and a hotel suite for two with full meals, ten dollars a day.

My attempts to show Ba that I was a strict moralist came up again when he asked me to buy some T-shirts in the U.S. military commissary for his son. I lectured him about such purchases being for U.S. military personnel only—although such a rule was interpreted with extreme laxity by all. In a few months I had learned enough about the good father under the fussy, contemptuous manner to present Ba with the T-shirts on the day of our leaving Saigon, earning a reluctant smile number two from him.

He became a different sort of man as more of his personal life impinged on ours, if only for brief emergency intervals. On the day that Johnson trounced Goldwater in one of the largest presidential victories in U.S. history, Ba approached us at dinner in high distress because one of his sons was in jail for stealing, for the second time. He showed us his son's school record with top marks. It was not clear whether he was arguing that such a good student could not possibly steal and was another victim of the incompetent Saigon police, or that conditions were so bad with his family that his son had to resort to thievery. In any case, the injustice of the arrest and the blow to his pride came searing through. We took his word for it. (Later that day, an American colleague who spoke Vietnamese went to the police station to inquire and got the boy released with consummate ease.)

Ba periodically threatened to quit during his six months with us because of a continuing war of wills with Chi Hai, number-one "boyesse," as the French called it. Chi Hai was a high-strung, angry woman in her early thirties, with a calculating expression on her pointed face and obvious ambitions to better herself and the one child she brought with her. This child was a chubby daughter of four who, with her mother's encouragement, spent all of her energies figuring out how to look cute. Both mother and daughter were ivory-skinned, with medium brown hair, the daughter's almost blond and curly.

Chi Hai often brought her daughter into the ground floor of the house and motioned toward her with meaningful smiles and nods of the head to direct my attention to the little girl. I reacted cooly to these overtures since the girl appeared obnoxious to me and I was not sure how much I was supposed to get involved with servants' personal lives. It is evident to me now that Chi Hai had been doing all she could to encourage such involvement. She often remarked that Madame looked nice with a suntan and freckles but that she and her daughter had to stay fair. She was vigilant in keeping the sun off her daughter's face with straw hats and parasols. She told me late in our stay that she had four children, the oldest one age eleven; that her father was a cook; and that she wanted this youngest daughter to go to a

French school and not be a "boyesse." She made no mention of a husband.

Her ambition for herself and her daughter was never far from the tense surface of her face. I did not appreciate her resourcefulness and determination to find a better place for herself in a profession and whole society growing increasingly more fragile. I felt that she was spying on me at the personal level and continually suspected her of going through my drawers when I was out, although I never found any evidence. I made overtures too. I took photographs of the two and opened discussions about Saigon life—both of us speaking a French that although not equally correct was equally fractured—while we watered the depressed houseplants in the living room or collected dirty laundry together upstairs. Chi Hai asserted each time that "La guerre est pas bon" and that the people had liked Diem better than Khanh.

She moved about industriously at keeping our living quarters clean, although the actual dusting, mopping, and sweeping were carried out by Chi Bai, a docile, plump older woman who took Chi Hai's peremptory tone and occasional nastiness with a cordial air. I considered it grossly unjust that Chi Bai did such a large share of the actual labor, but both women were operating within a system that I had not fathomed.

Chi Hai's firm ideas on social place and behavior extended to our dinner table guests. One Monday evening, a freewheeling German acquaintance who had declared himself to have "gone native" brought a thin Vietnamese girl who alternately fidgeted and languished at the dinner table behind long, straight black hair. She obviously could not understand the conversation and, judging by Chi Hai's sullen looks in serving her, she was probably of that burgeoning profession, a bar girl. Chi Hai contributed to her discomfort by grabbing the plates before the girl was clearly finished and making sure to serve her each course last.

An even ruder incident occurred when a distinguished Vietnamese diplomat appeared at our driveway gate in his tennis clothes, stopping by on his way back from a game at Le Cercle Sportif Saigonais. Chi Hai refused to let him in, telling him brusquely that we were not at home and that she would not forward a message. I was never clear whether her disapproval focused on the man's politics, sweaty attire, or sun-darkened skin.

The sweaty attire as a possible culprit reappeared in a third incident, when Chi Hai refused to refill the glass of an American journalist friend who had come to dinner directly from Bien-hoa air base the day after a Viet Cong surprise attack destroyed several bombers and killed Americans and Vietnamese. Our friend was dressed in his dirty, many-pocketed khaki combat shirt, muddy boots, and heavy-duty wristwatch. Perhaps Chi Hai was expressing her general distaste for reminders of the war. (This journalist was later shot down in the plane of a Vietnamese general for whom he was writing a history.)

It was not a mystery why Chi Hai and Ba did not get along. He considered her overbearing and interfering and she disliked his fussy and humorless way of directing the show. They were both tense and strong-willed. This showed particularly in the two deep lines between Chi Hai's eyebrows, which she accentuated by squeezing hard to alleviate her frequent headaches. She urged such a remedy on me, claiming that it pressed out the pain.

As the end of our stay drew near, we noticed that both Ba and Chi Hai were speaking more English, in expectation that their next employers would be American. We found Chi Hai a position with Chinese-American acquaintances who were serving with USIA in Saigon. We heard from them years later that she had been impossible—slovenly, rude, incompetent, surly. Possibly the historical Vietnamese animosity toward the Chinese rose to the surface in Chi Hai, and perhaps she was beginning to fall apart under the stress of working in a position that was losing its stability in the overheated atmosphere of Saigon life—and that ill-suited her dreams for her daughter.

The day we left Saigon, Ba and Chi Hai came to the airport to say good-bye. I handed him the T-shirts and gave her a commissary Christmas stocking filled with toys and a Thai black star sapphire pendant for herself. She looked pleased.

Rue Catinat and Others

The main street of Saigon had been named Catinat by the French, the same name as their warship that steamed into Tourane (now Da Nang) in September 1856, destroyed the harbor forts, and landed marines to force Emperor Tu Doc to cede the city to France. In March 1965, the first American combat troops, also marines, arrived in Vietnam at the same spot. The street name Catinat had been changed in the early 1960s to Tu Do, Freedom, but the old name was the one most people were still using.

The streets where we walked in Saigon covered a small area about six blocks long, between our house and the Saigon River. If going anywhere else, we were advised to take one of the ubiquitous battered taxis or, as second choice, a bicycle-driven *cyclopousse* so as not to call attention to ourselves and provoke outbursts of hostility. Another factor was the heat and humidity of the street, which by midday rendered us dripping wet, beginning in the scalp and running down to the toes. Around the corner from our residential street and standing at the head of Rue Catinat was the Saigon Cathedral, a musty redbrick church with modest twin steeples and the hazy facade of Monet's Rouen Cathedral—hazy because the building was set in an open plaza that collected the city's heat and bad air. The plaza was renamed Kennedy Square after the assassination of the President in November 1963. The cathedral was active, both inside—for the city's substantial number of practicing Catholics—and outside—for the men and women hunkering down in the plaza area for conversation and a bowl of noodle soup.

The clearest sign that the city was stretched beyond its population capacity was the traffic and noise of its streets, built for quieter, more gracious times. The blue air from motor scooters, military trucks, idling passenger cars, and unmufflered taxis and small commercial vans rose beyond our nostrils and above the tops of the eucalyptus trees lining the boulevards. Drivers leaned on their horns as a matter of course, staring straight ahead with a blind impassivity that implied there was no one else on the road. In the most precarious position were the vendors traveling on the streets by bicycle or foot, suspending their goods from long poles tied to their backs—although I never saw one of these people in an actual accident. Simply walking was not so hazardous, and the wide brick sidewalks provided a little more free breathing space.

Past the cathedral and a small green park began the hotel and shopping section of Rue Catinat. The Hotel Continental, still under French management at the time, served drinks on a long, wide veranda that was a traditional target for terrorist bombs. A few yards farther down was the new Caravelle Hotel, with its bar that was famous as the roosting place for journalists trading stories about the war. At the bottom of the street was the decorous Majestic Hotel where we first stayed, overlooking the dark and sullen Saigon River. The hotel had lacy bronze elevator cages operated by white-gloved lift boys. Above the ground-floor bar and restaurant were high-ceilinged rooms with wide four-poster beds curtained by mosquito netting, heavy flowered drapes, and a plethora of service people walking in at any hour without knocking to change towels or shine shoes. The maître d', with a formal and distinguished air, acknowledged that he remembered Joe from four years earlier. With heavy silver and linen napkins, he served a breakfast of delicately vinegared, perfectly timed poached eggs, thin toast, and halved papaya with slices of lime.

The shops and sidewalk bars along Catinat were filled with Westerners as well as Vietnamese. Some of them shopped with great intensity, particularly the women in French-style tight skirts and silk dresses or in the traditional *ao dai,* tapping authoritatively through the shop doors in high heels. Swaying along in groups of twos and threes, American soldiers ducked in and out of doorways, with their good-natured grins and easy spending money.

They were the sole focus of very young bar girls with smiling faces and somber eyes. In a different kind of uniform were the students, all in white tieless shirts and dark trousers, sitting at tables or walking in groups of five or more abreast, talking only to each other and intent on some mission other than shopping. Clusters of men in casual dress or journalist battle fatigues walked along unseeing, speaking animatedly on important subjects.

A little less busy with modern commercial enterprises was a parallel street—the one other that we walked regularly—called Nguyen Hue. It was a wide, tree-lined boulevard of high commercial office buildings and apartments and a traditional Vietnamese central market: long islands of flower stalls down the center, soup vendors, outdoor barbers and dentists, supplies and appliances obtained from the U.S. military commissary and sold on the black market by squatting men and women in straw hats spreading their wares on the sidewalks. Parades and public demonstrations usually marched down this street because at the other end were the official buildings of the South Vietnamese government—the Saigon City Hall fronted by a large plaza; several blocks and to the right, the National Assembly (built by the French as an opera house); and a few blocks farther, the Presidential Palace and the Hall of Justice.

Beggars

My biggest problem in walking down the street was beggars. I was not prepared either for them or my own shocking reaction to them, which I am still hard put to explain. Saigon beggars were mostly children, some crippled, or, we were informed, maimed and often diseased. Others looked simply poor, and some had no sign of beggardom other than practiced beseeching voices and gestures. All were horribly aggressive. Combined with their fawning gestures was a square meeting of your eyes and a ferocious persistence that made walking along certain sidewalks impossible for Western, particularly American, newcomers.

There was one legless nine-year-old boy whom I regularly avoided. He pushed himself on a skateboard with great speed and agility, between the Hotel Continental—where he operated among the tables on the veranda—and the Caravelle. He rolled among newsmen and visitors who were arranging airline tickets in the ground-floor travel office of the Caravelle. Another, a woman who chewed and spit out betel nut between red teeth, sent out three children with running eyes and severed limbs every morning from her home of sidewalk rags across from the Continental.

My reaction to being latched onto by one of these degraded human beings was total fury, followed by a contemptuous sarcasm that remains shameful in memory. One afternoon I went to the Central Market with Chi Hai to buy some vases. The market to me was never pleasant—hot, crowded, continual haggling, full of rotting fish and vegetable smells. One ragged girl of about ten, who had just been chasing around with a friend, pulled down her face, pulled my arm, and held out her hand, which had a few piasters in it given by others. I took one, said with a false smile, "Thank you very much," and pretended to put it in my pocket. She looked confused and I felt at the time I had made some obscure point.

Another day on the same street, a healthy-looking boy followed along for two blocks asking in a low whine for money. With a combination of exasperation and ill will, I ripped the small cellophane cover off a pack of gum and put the crinkly piece of paper in his outstretched hand. For a few seconds, he stared at it, then looked me brightly in the eye and laughed. He turned the paper over and over in mock wonder and pressed it to his face with noises of false gratitude. I laughed with him.

What is the explanation for such bizarre behavior on my part? In both incidents, I remember a desperate need to escape the level of pretense and degradation in which I was being invited to participate. Perhaps that is why my instinct was to laugh ironically with these children at the bitter level of relationship into which Saigon life had thrown us. The boy with the cellophane seemed to have shared that feeling for the few minutes that he did his fake gratitude act. I recognized the same defusing irony twenty-four years later when a pickpocket in New York City lifted my wallet out of my purse as I was walking down a packed Times Square street. I turned around at feeling my purse lighten on my shoulder, caught him lifting out my wallet by the corner, and, without reflecting or looking him in the eye, smiled and held out my hand. He politely put the wallet back in my hand and said, "Oh, excuse me." "That's quite all right," I answered, and we quietly parted, like slight acquaintances who had just exchanged remarks on the weather.

Saigon beggary provoked in me a mixture of shock at seeing such physical ruin in children, anger at the con game playing on real misery, and fury at the injustice of my being held personally accountable. But deep inside another voice murmured to me every day I walked down the streets of Saigon that I had somehow played a part in producing these sorry human beings.

Wives

Living with compatriots in a foreign place can be a cushion against culture shock but also an opportunity to see one's country in a new way, particularly in the complex self-image presented to Americans living in Saigon in 1964. Coupled with the attractions and repulsions of an exotic subtropical Southeast Asian city was a pervasive feeling among Americans of having a mission to fulfill. We considered it inappropriate and unjust to describe this mission as colonial, an immediate association with the methods and failures of our French predecessors. We preferred "democratization" and "nation building." The ambiguity of this mission pervaded the relationships among American women living in Saigon, who, with few exceptions, reflected their husbands' particular notions of what that mission was.

For a time, my closest acquaintance—it was difficult to consider anyone a friend in such an unstable and temporary setting—worked in the project and was the wife of an American intelligence officer. By the time of our arrival, she had already been in Saigon a few months and had set up a comfortable house with a genial servant and a friendly puppy. She also had determined what needed to be changed in the place. We had animated discussions in which she provided me with a number of forcefully worded opinions on Vietnam: that almost everyone was poor and regarded life as of little value; that babies did not have the health and good looks of American infants; that the differences between rich and poor made for constant danger in the streets and even in the home because the poor coveted the goods of the rich and, she added, had a right to them.

She expressed impatience and contempt for the machinations of the Saigon government and pronounced it a rotten system that needed to learn much more from ours. But she also asserted that the heavy presence of foreigners in Saigon was corrupting the place. She considered herself an international citizen, not rooted in any one culture. We shared a propensity for frank speaking, which she said she found to be her best weapon against snide remarks. What she and her husband missed most about the States was the opportunity to drive twenty miles to a lake and stretch out. What she missed least were people who were opinionated when they did not know what they were talking about.

The toughest and most resigned bunch was the wives of American military officers. I spent one afternoon playing bridge with such a group, who impressed me with their leathery faces, accomplished bridge skills, and humorous sarcasm about servants and shopping. Their remarks were untainted by a single complaint about being in Saigon or by a mention of the seething political climate around them. One of these wives, a Texan with dark gray hair, large white jewelry, and conversation doused with curses, had lived in Saigon for seven years and advised me to buy a Yamaha piano through the commissary and ship it back home.

Another acquaintance of a different kind of brashness was the young resident wife of a UPI correspondent, who joined her husband in attacking the U.S. military at every opportunity.

The diplomatic corps was in Saigon to ameliorate South Vietnamese–American relations, of course, and therefore had to put on a softer front. In a similar position was one woman, a New Yorker with long experience living abroad as the wife of a U.S. military contractor, who considered me her protégée. There began a highly uncomfortable relationship that was bound to fail. She was twitchy, excessively sensitive, and aggressive, approaching people with warm words and a discontented expression around her mouth, sometimes turning away abruptly as if her feelings had been bruised. She always took care to introduce me to people—in an embarrassingly aggressive manner—and suggested taking me to events she sensed I would enjoy, like a student concert of traditional Vietnamese music. But she made it almost impossible to accept her overtures with grace because of her unbearably tense manner.

Of all the wives I met in Saigon, she was probably the most open and eager to immerse herself in the culture of Vietnam, but her expressions of that impulse took some peculiar turns, which at the time I found shocking. She had a fragile-looking daughter of about six to whom she and her husband spoke only French (although both were Americans). She explained that this was so the little girl would learn that language at the formative age. Her daughter never spoke English because she attended a French-language school and was being cared for exclusively by a Vietnamese nanny whose French was so sparse that she mixed it liberally with Vietnamese. The last time I saw my would-be protector she was due to give birth to a second child whom she evidently intended to raise in the same manner.

Two women who were not wives and who were serving in missions outside the U. S. government stand apart from the others. The first, a Canadian, was a soft-spoken and delicate-looking woman with an elegant manner of speaking and deep and determined seriousness. She was single-handedly directing a social-service agency in South Vietnam that provided child care, medical help, schooling, and job training to poor families—this amid the turmoil and civil war and governments toppling around her.

It was during a reception at her house and clinic on the road to Tan Son Nhut airport that I met the second woman. I sat down next to a tall blond American with upswept hair and idly asked her where she was from. She assured me I would never have heard of such a small town; I assured her that the same applied to my hometown—and then we astounded each other with the discovery that it was the same place. It was one of those eerie moments when the everyday world stands still and coincidence envelops you with an intense joy and mysterious significance out of all proportion to the event itself.

Arts

There was a young artist in her twenties whose pictures of traditional Vietnam were popular with Americans in Saigon, probably because of the cartoon quality and the light, easy tone of her work. She signed her pictures Beky, which further endeared her to Americans and was probably an elision of her Vietnamese names. Using the materials of Chinese brush painting, she did multitudes of quick sketches—usually black ink on white rice paper or silk—of children sitting on buffaloes' backs, sidewalk barbers and dentists, sampans gliding down rivers under bending bamboo stalks, and children playing street games. Her portfolio was vaguely reminiscent of classical Chinese paintings of animals and flowers, without their exquisite brushwork and powerful use of white space and isolated detail.

I first saw some Bekys at a USAID Tea and was convinced by the hostess that they were charming. The artist came to our house the next morning with a full portfolio. I then decided that her work was not only charming but sophisticated, so I purchased eight small ones on the spot and commissioned one long, horizontal panel of the Vietnam countryside, in color. The latter turned out to be disappointingly flat and lifeless, despite its multitude of peasants in various postures of labor and leisure. Her talents lay more with the quick fragment than with the complex and panoramic.

I pretended to be delighted with the large picture because dealing with Beky required that one be solicitous. She had an intelligent, plain face and careless dress and was surprisingly anxious and serious for one who produced such lightweight work. During our discussion about the large countryside panel, she wrote down my vague suggestions for subject matter with a deferential but distracted air and a disconcerting half smile. She left me with the uncomfortable conclusion that hidden beneath the facile brushstrokes was either a more disturbing kind of artist or a member of a secret political group. Much more satisfying than her paintings were the handsome black and white frames in which they were mounted, built by a straightforward Chinese student with excellent English who ran a shop in Saigon and hoped to emigrate to Hong Kong.

The only other art I purchased in Saigon was a Rouault-style still life in oils hanging at a student exhibit. When I look now at the standard flowers and fruit, rendered with gobs of yellow paint and heavy black outlines, I wonder why the painting struck me back then as in any way remarkable or at all representative of that time and place.

There were also traditional-style Vietnamese paintings on lacquer and wooden boxes and silk cloth displayed in the Saigon shops, but these were garish and crude. On the other hand, the subtle dark brown and gray spiked mountains of the Chinese painter exhibiting one morning at a neighbor's home seemed completely remote and irrelevant.

Fauna

Attachment to household pets was rarely in evidence among residents of preoccupied Saigon. Our immediate neighbors protected their houses and cars with hidden, chained beasts that, judging by the deepness and ferocity of their barks, must have been German shepherds. I do not remember seeing any dogs being walked. The one Vietnamese neighbor I actually visited—in order to use her piano—had three small white lapdogs of the Chinese traditional painting variety who suffered from an unsightly mange that distressed their owner more for its ugliness than its effect on the animals. Chi Hai and Chi Bai regularly remarked that the appearance and disappearance of various small dogs at a house down the street was due to their serving as regular household cuisine rather than pets—a common practice, I was assured, of both the North Vietnamese and the Chinese.

I remember seeing no cats at all, although the size of the rats caught at intervals in our back storm drains by the military maintenance crew suggested that a cat population, of the large variety, would serve the city well. Because of the trees and flowers constantly blooming throughout Saigon, I would like to imagine exotic birds and bird songs outside our windows—but again, I cannot remember a single instance of noticing a bird, not even rude, sharp-witted crows, for which I have a special fondness.

Ponies and bulls with jutting rib cages hauled firewood and produce over the streets. In the marketplace, mournful trick monkeys sometimes could be seen on the shoulders of their owners, trying to attract children, and once a vendor was selling a long, beautiful striped wildcat in a rhinestone collar, obviously ill and doped. When I remarked "Il est malade," the vendor glowered at me and shook the leash to stir the animal to sit up. The small Saigon zoo was well designed for spacious family walking and cultivated greenery, with paths winding past a small number of cages. The best event was the sight of the odd-looking black bears with half-pig, half-ape faces, wrestling gracefully like lazy fat men.

The insect population was fertile, ubiquitous, and the focus of attention for Americans particularly—in their rejection of the old colonial mosquito netting and demand that all windows be screened. Adjustment was an active challenge. According to an old saying, the first year in Saigon, you order another glass when a fly is found in your drink. The second year, you remove the fly before drinking. The third year, you drink it, fly and all, and find it tasty that way. Most women occupied themselves at lawn dinner parties by swatting their legs. The best friends to the bitten were the multisized ghekkos—tan lizards ranging from one or two inches to over one foot who lived along the inside and outside of our walls and ceilings. They made satisfying clicking noises like Fisher-Price toys and rapidly depleted the bug population with darting tongues. They were an attractive, skittish bunch that I tried to keep out of our air-conditioned bedroom because they could not survive in such cold air. The other source of natural music was a Vietnamese variety of cricket or locust that made the pleasing chirping we associate with summer nights.

Our most intimate experience with the fauna of Vietnam was one horseback-riding episode in Da Lat, a mountain town a short plane ride from Saigon. The French innkeeper where we stayed was puzzled at our shorts, long socks, and tennis shoes and at our request for trail-riding horses. At our insistence, he sent us to a herdsman who laughed, took our payment, and helped us aboard two small gray ponies with sagging backs. The ponies jogged reluctantly up and down a few scraggy hills, moving only because their owner ran after them with a switch. A small crowd of country people gathered to watch and giggle. They were complimenting me, the owner claimed, on my good seat when the ride abruptly ended with a cartoon flourish because Joe's groaning pony sat down like a camel and refused to move. (On that same day, in Saigon, Generals Lam Van Phat and Duong Van Duc led a coup against the Khanh government, which they then canceled the next day under American pressure and the threat of bombardment by Air Vice Marshal Nguyen Cao Ky.)

Flora

Each Saigon fruit had its own passionate personality. The most ravishing in appearance looked like a banana with a bulge. It had a bubble-gum-pink rind opening to a black and white striped fruit with flat, shiny black seeds that had to be removed delicately one by one with the point of a sharp knife. The taste was surprisingly mild after all the fireworks, and forgettable. The pomme canelle was almost as garish—a chartreuse tennis ball with large raised warts—with sweet, spicy inside meat that quickly became mushy if not cut open soon enough. The mangosteen had a dark burgundy pulpy casing concealing a small white tangerine that combined the taste of a lime and an orange. This delectable fruit was our most frequent luncheon dessert, not any less desirable because of the care with which the soft casing had to be pared off without puncturing the delicate sections inside.

The heaviest taste, almost like meat, was the dark orange fruit of the mango, which I asserted in an ongoing argument was inferior to the papaya. The latter was my favorite. It does not have the mango's slightly rotting smell and obtrusive pit strung with tough fibers that always got caught between the teeth. The papaya has a generous and benevolent nature, edible from top of slice to bottom rind. After one sweep of the small black glutinous seeds on top and another sweep of juice from a fresh lime slice, your spoon is free to dig into the whole tender, sweet golden orange fruit that slips down easily and makes you glad you are in the tropics.

The Saigon pomplemousse, a cousin to our grapefruit, had some of the properties of a desert succulent, with the rind of a rhinoceros and globules of juice stored in a thick, translucent skin like bottles in a wine cellar. When your teeth broke through these, your mouth was flooded with a light, tart juice that was particularly refreshing with a sugary pastry. The bananas were sometimes dark red and small rather than our long yellow variety, or other times light green, but both kinds were firm and sweet with a drying consistency that pulled at the mouth slightly.

The look and taste of the pineapple was totally familiar, the most important aspect of that fruit being that I learned to cut it expeditiously. With a wide machetelike knife, Ba cut off the ends, sliced it lengthwise in quarters, swooped off the pale woody strip along the top of each quarter, and scooped the fruit away from the rind. He then cut up each quarter in bite-size pieces served in the rind like boats of gold bars. My favorite part was the juicy, mushy fruit sticking to the rind, which yielded to hard scrapes with a spoon.

The most sinister fruit was the dorian, which sat like a big green bomb in the marketplace and emitted the odor of a stable in midsummer with no breeze. This imposing outside was obviously only a front to discourage predators. Inside, the fruit was surprisingly mild, smooth, and delicate.

Eating Saigon fruit concentrated the mind and senses, to the exclusion of any other concern. Arguments about whether the United States should bomb the North or intimate stories about private lives would pause until seeds and rind had been removed and everyone had taken the first few bites. Other food did not have quite that same power of arresting worldly concerns. It is the contexts in which they were served, not their tastes, that remain.

There were the French-style dinners that Ba was most proud of serving—beef or chicken in wine sauces, lobster filets and buttery vegetables, and crepes and fruit tarts. The Vietnamese dinners of steaming noodles and rolled vegetables and ground meat and fish in spicy sauces were set perfunctorily on the table, our rave reactions greeted with a skeptical nod. For one cocktail party, he spent two days directing his wife and children in all the chopping, cooking, and wrapping needed to serve Vietnamese hors d'oeuvres, accompanied by slivers of anchovy pizza, pineapple and cheese slices toothpicked into a pineapple, and shrimp speared into a cabbage. The Thanksgiving dinner he created was almost perfectly traditional, including a sweet-potato casserole with raisins, and cranberry and orange relish. The only strange note was the eggnog served as hors d'oeuvre, like a dinner guest who had gotten the date wrong.

The only two snacks within recall are the sugary French ice cream we served after a chamber-music evening in our living room and one midnight snack consisting incredibly of banana pie, blue cheese, and red wine. One afternoon at the British Ladies' Commissary Charity Sale, among pleasant voices chirping about how difficult it was to find good beef, I bought mint vinaigrette sauce, orange marmalade, biscuits, and tea, and met a French woman whose family name, Braquebien, sounded like a candy company. There were the dinners at the homes of French-educated Vietnamese, usually with overabundant menus. One such couple who had their money in a French bank and soon were to depart for Paris presented us with soup, quiche, stuffed fish, roast chicken in a cream-wine sauce, fruit, four kinds of pie, ice cream, wines, champagne—served with the bitter complaints of our host and hostess regarding their life in Saigon.

Of course, there were the one or two days of noneating due to a bout of common dysentery, when I slept most of the day and dined on toast, tea, and soup broth.

There was only one drink in Saigon I can still taste: the iced Italian sweet vermouth with lemon peel poured by a French journalist writing for the American press. At a small dinner party on a balcony overlooking Rue Catinat, he and several other old Vietnam hands barely contained their pessimism about the course of the war. A while later, he was killed in a plane crash over central Vietnam while on a press mission.

Tennis Student

Saigon tropical heat made tennis an activity only for the hardy—and, in my case, for those stumbling upon an irresistible personal challenge. The place was a defunct tennis club, Le Cercle Sportif Vietnamien, superceded by the newer, posher Cercle Sportif Saigonais. This older club comprised a few cracked cement courts that radiated a great deal of heat, attended by a sickly man in a torn straw hat who lived with his children—the club ball boys—in a shack beside the center court. A few professional-looking Vietnamese in tennis whites strolled around from time to time giving advice and, less frequently, playing a few sets.

The attendant was the only one there consistently and since no one was in charge of setting a policy for new members, we set our own terms and schedule, paying the attendant a few piasters an hour for the time and trouble we put him to. I arranged to hit with him for an hour three or four days a week, usually at 8:30 A.M., before the sun became murderous.

This fragile-looking man (whose name I never asked until the last week) soon proved to be an intelligent and agile trainer, speaking no French or English but giving steady returns from all angles of the court and demonstrating the proper strokes with his own bulky wooden racket. He looked sad on the days when my sweat and blisters only resulted in frustration and a relentless inconsistency, and smiled briefly and curtly nodded his straw hat when three returns in a row were satisfactorily executed. He was always patient with my need to anlayze each kind of stroke into its several parts, reserving his negative expressions exclusively for his small sons, who were constantly coughing and running at the eyes and nose as they retrieved the balls for us.

My diary notes of those hot days are filled with exhortations to improve and small pats on the back when I did. Some free advice was provided by the few elderly spectators in immaculate white who occasionally came over and complimented me in elegant French on my American-style blue shorts and striped jerseys—which I took as a veiled criticism—and offered to demonstrate the backhand. One claimed that he had coached the Davis Cup team for Vietnam and he took over a few sessions to show me the net game. The trainer watched these sessions from his shack with a proprietary, disgusted air. He explained later, by demonstration, that the coach was too old to hit from the back court.

I have often wondered since what he thought of this serious young American sweating through a routine that made halting progress and that had no apparent goal of ever actually playing the game, only of chasing after the perfect form. I used to wonder whether under that bland exterior there was seething resentment of my health and privilege and the paltry amount we were paying him. He had a deep cough and caved-in chest, not helped by the chain of strong-smelling cigarettes he smoked during idle hours. At the time, my own rigid code of conduct between trainer and student—imported inappropriately from home—prevented me from acting more generously toward him. But he exhibited only professional seriousness and somber dignity. He never asked for favors and only once for an advance in pay because his wife was ill.

English Teacher

The Vietnamese American Association was sponsored by the U.S. Information Agency and provided to Saigon residents an adult-education center where I taught English three days a week. Taxi drivers, shop owners, university students, civil servants, bar girls, French and Japanese wives of officials and businessmen—all attended English classes because they saw their fates linked with the Americans.

The VAA was housed in a two-story painted cement building. The assistant director, a rosy-cheeked Mexican woman dressed in an *ao dai,* had a constant radiant smile for anyone who walked through the gate. My course of study was to hold rigorously to a total immersion workbook organized around oral repetition of phrases and conversations, written exercises, and simply drawn illustrations. The idea was to focus exclusively on conversation so that students would be out and speaking at the end of each two-month session. Although such a method seemed to promise tedious teaching, the students' response changed the nature of the whole exercise.

In addition to the gratification of helping eager students improve, there was also a creeping realization, more in retrospect, that I might be helping some of these people find a way out of a darkening present. But, again in retrospect, stirring such hopes may also have been a disservice to those who did not leave Saigon after its fall.

In any case, what has remained of those hot mornings of classroom exercises is a pool of intent faces, some hiding behind shy hands over their mouths, and upright postures, repeating after me in singsong voices, "Let's have a party. We're going to have a party. We're going to have a party tomorrow night." The two classes I taught differed in level of difficulty but followed the same lesson plan. At first, in my eagerness to hold their interest, I gave too many complicated explanations for such strange English phenomena as contractions and tense differentiation, which probably seemed relevant only to those students who had studied French. On the other hand, explaining the book illustrations of Halloween and football and Columbus Day held their interest and demanded that I adapt these strange rituals to their vocabulary level in English.

They were most delighted when one morning I made a mistake in the order of sentences I was repeating. I made sure to do this again from time to time so we could all laugh at the simpleminded severity of the method. Usually, a few students stayed afterward, asking me pointedly how I pronounced my name, or more expansively (sometimes in French) why I was in Vietnam and whether I had children. The political world of Saigon never intruded in this schoolroom except for the class days following street riots, when fewer students than usual appeared.

The lower-level class included two middle-aged Japanese women who sat together in the front row and responded forcefully to the oral drill work but were terribly pained when asked to speak alone. An expensively dressed French woman felt no such scruples but only showed up for two classes. One Vietnamese matron who always listened with a sympathetic but vague expression often drove me home in a large black Citroën with her two children. In a second-term class, an eager Chinese boy whose occupation I never determined enjoyed inventing alternative sentence constructions and offering them for our amusement. No one else in the class followed his lead.

One Vietnamese who was obviously impatient with the class method always spoke after class at length in French. I can no longer bring to mind the subject except that he was intensely literary. The most amazing student was a blind boy of about eighteen, tall and thin with a dreaming face. He brought a raised picture book to class, which he read with his fingers while listening and repeating our relentless oral drill. He took his final exam by responding in braille to the questions and then reading his answers to me after class. His face shone when he got a perfect score and he remarked that this was the first time a teacher at the VAA had given him an examination.

Le Cercle Hippique

A month before our departure, the day we purchased our return plane tickets, I started riding lessons at Le Cercle Hippique. Although it seemed like an aimless enterprise not likely to be continued back home, I looked forward each day to entering the dowdy atmosphere of the place, closed away from frenetic Saigon, where I could pretend that the sturdy horses munching in their stalls were all anticipating my arrival and my determination to find a secure seat at the canter.

The half-deserted club was on a side street, and had a stable of about ten horses and about the same number of club members. There were signs of former better days. A large outdoor ring, unused and overgrown with flower bushes and tall spiked grass, opened out from an indoor ring, cool, with soft, dusty turf and muffled sound under a high wooden beamed ceiling. An observation balcony still had part of its glass window where judges used to view shows and competitions. Outside, in two long shed rows of box stalls, compact horses identified by the riding instructor as Australian ponies were cared for with a desultory, cheerless air by a few elderly Vietnamese grooms.

There were two riding instructors on duty. One was a French woman whose only traits I remember are iron-gray hair and a harsh voice shouting many-syllabled commands in French to her two young students. The younger student, a boy of eight or nine, holding on to the reins with white knuckles and a white face, was followed around the ring on foot by his Vietnamese chauffeur, who was in turn followed on foot by the boy's mother, gesturing to the chauffeur and calling to him again and again: *"Laisse-le, laisse-le!"*

At the same time, instruction in English was conducted by an American army captain who gruffly provided advice both on riding and on building character. Evidently, his other student, a teenage American boy who had played polo in Thailand, needed almost no guidance from the captain, so all his guns were turned on me. I undoubtedly needed the advice, since—as the captain told me the first day—I was not doing anything right. Toes down, weak legs, bouncing seat, and arbitrary signals resulted in a balky horse and a lot of puffing on my part. Then came the subsequent days of elation at my control of myself and my horse—and disgust when it fled.

My favorite horse was a medium-size chestnut mare named Babsy. She was the most difficult to ride at my stage of development but hinted at a certain sensitivity that challenged me to sit well so she would canter in a neat circle instead of charging into a standstill at the corners. Her groom was attached to her and scowled if I brought her back in too much of a nervous sweat. Babsy probably sensed the decay and instability of her present workplace and was having thoughts of moving on, which inevitably encourages a less sanguine attitude toward one's job. In the photograph we took of her, she is standing under a large tree outside her stall, with the sun on her chestnut coat and a resigned but thoughtful look on her face.

Over those few weeks, the captain barked out his orders to volt and half-volt and told me that no one reaches peak form until after fifty because good riding is really self-discipline. Despite the fact that my sweat and determination were not leading clearly toward progress, I drank in the obsolete air of the place, combining equine and French elegance, and felt myself in training for some obscure future line of duty.

In Concert

Soon after we moved into our house, I rented a piano. It must have been the overheated atmosphere of our Saigon existence that created this sudden thirst for playing classical music. Every day I played for hours during the cool time—relentless Bach preludes and fugues, Chopin études, a Mozart concerto that always got most exciting at the wrenching modulations. Then there was the piano trio music that needed to be practiced for my French partners, particularly the second movement of the Schubert trio, the cellist's favorite.

Finding a piano to buy or rent was not easy. I followed one tip to a piano factory in Cholon, the Chinese section, where an old man in a pith helmet wrapped in smoke rings from his cigarette assembled pianos with the help of several children. They worked in a narrow, dark room, more of a hallway, piled with keyboards, legs, music racks, soundboards, lids, nails, and glue. There were no whole pianos visible, and after trying to ask a few questions and being greeted with blank stares, I left quickly in dismay. The children laughed at my bumbling manner when I hurried back into the taxi.

I rented an old dark brown Hansen upright at 1,100 piasters a month ($15 U.S.), with a 5,000 piasters security deposit, from a crotchety old Vietnamese woman whose French was more uncertain than mine. She became so upset over something she thought I had said that we had to spend a half hour more repeating ourselves to straighten it out. The next day, as promised, the piano arrived on the back of a pickup truck. It fit exactly between the barred side windows and wall lights of our living room, except for a slight tipping of the back end because of the floor molding.

Before renting a piano, I borrowed one. The day after Congress had passed the Gulf of Tonkin Resolution and we began bombing North Vietnam's bases, I met a young Vietnamese woman who lived in a large cream-colored cement apartment complex around the corner, owned by her family. She was a concert pianist trained at a Paris conservatory and she agreed to let me play on her twin black concert grands, Yamahas, sitting back to back in a large airy room of her third-floor apartment. The room had three wooden and flower-cushioned sofas, two chairs with plastic-covered seats, and potted plants and flowers. There were only three lamps—one over the pianos and two underneath to cut the dampness. A picture of Mary Baker Eddy was on the wall. The long expanse of pinkish tile floor opened onto a balcony over the inner court of the building, always crowded with drying laundry, maids playing with boisterous children, and vertical cages full of small songbirds, the favorites of the landlady. The family pets, three small long-haired white dogs suffering from mange, waddled in and out the heavy wooden double doors behind their mistress's heels when she came in to talk to me as I played over Bach, Chopin, and Mozart.

My hostess was always dressed like a cinema version of a Sorbonne student, in a gray turtleneck sweater and dark pants, long hair in no particular style falling beside a somber face. She spoke in short bursts whether in English or French and we were never able to carry on a conversation with any continuity to it. Her often surprising remarks about herself were raised and dropped abruptly, giving her whole person a cryptic quality. One day she mentioned that she played Tchaikovsky's Piano Concerto for eight hours straight as the background for a film. At another time she pointed to the Eddy picture on the wall and stated simply, apropos of nothing, that she was a Christian Scientist.

On the second day of my visit to her pianos, in mid-August, she glided through the doors with her dogs and asked me to share a benefit recital with her. The concert was to be sponsored by the Gray Ladies, a volunteer group of Saigon wives of senior Vietnamese military officers whose purpose was to do good works for the victims of the war. My hostess needed a piano accompaniment for her performance of the Mozart Piano Concerto in A Major and also needed a soloist to share the program with her; I was invited to play two or three pieces of my own. I chose Chopin's *Black Key Etude,* a Bach prelude and fugue, and a humorous Roy Harris suite. My partner would supplement the Mozart concerto with three Romantics—Debussy, Liszt, and Fauré.

I practiced with enthusiasm over the next three months— at first at my partner's house or at a small conservatory near the Saigon Cathedral—in a relaxed frame of mind because I assumed that the audience would be uncritical. My partner appeared less frequently and often canceled our practice sessions together, leaving me puzzled as to whether she was tense or blasé about the approaching performance.

We had critics of various levels of severity listening to us during our practice sessions. My partner's husband, who was in the South Vietnamese navy, commented vaguely, with a genteel manner and good English and French. Her mother, in a long traditional dress, floated in several times and smiled, then left. Her father—who had just declined an invitation to be a minister in the short-lived Phan Khac Suu government—and a lawyer friend both bowed and smiled politely. Once while I was practicing at the conservatory, a boy came in and drew a picture of the piano and me for a program cover. Another time, a girl of about eight sat at the door for fifteen minutes, then indicated with a smile and graceful hand motions that it was her turn to use the piano.

A half-blind Czech music instructor listened to us play the Mozart and advised sourly that we practice together at least twenty more times. He would be writing the review of the concert for the local French-language newspaper. My partner's uncle listened without a word or gesture to one of our final practices. Two days before the recital, a small man dressed in a French-cut suit and well-shined shoes, and introduced only as M. Tuong, pronounced our rendition of the Mozart as "pas mal" but asserted cheerfully that Mozart could be played only by men.

The recital was canceled several times and revived, apparently due to the street demonstrations in Saigon, or more to the point, the anxiety on the part of the Gray Ladies chairwoman that she would not be able to sell enough tickets. The chairwoman, fidgety, with long, glossy fingernails, was ill-suited for her position, continually at a loss in making managerial decisions both before and at the concert. It was obvious that this benefit recital was not being presented for its artistic merit. It was, rather, a ceremonial demonstration that the Saigon upper class was contributing to the war effort.

For all the uncertainty in the planning stages, the event passed smoothly and with élan. The Vietnamese-French woman who did my hair had invented a new style for the occasion, with a sweeping cap and a forward curl over the ears. Our confused preliminary discussion of where to place lights, pianos, stools, flowers, bouquet presenters, announcers, and photographers was resolved by two fast-moving crew members who made the final moves without consulting anyone. The Gray Ladies—actually in blue nurse's uniforms and caps—chirped together proudly, some of them rehearsing their ceremonial speeches to be given at intermission. The only glitch was a bounding photographer who leapt about the stage during our performance and popped flashbulbs in our faces. My partner ignored him with professional cool and I followed suit, grateful afterward for the pictures.

About three hundred people attended—Vietnamese, Americans, and French—including many children. They applauded each number loudly and made gracious remarks afterward, including an effusive M. Tuong, who found the Mozart tolerable even though rendered by two women. Some said they were touched to see such a Vietnamese-American partnership. Mrs. Westmoreland sat in the front row. My riding instructor, the U.S. Army captain, sat silently in the back, and Chi Hai walked in late with her children, all dressed in flowered silks and straw hats.

The music had its effect in carrying us all out of Saigon for an hour and a half. My partner had abandoned her choppy and mechanical rehearsal Mozart for a nuanced interpretation at the right tempo, and this made up for the occasional mistakes. I regretted reaching the final chords of the Harris suite, which worked well as the final number. The next day in the French-language newspaper, our Czech critic wrote that I played agreeably and with sensitivity. But he regretted that since I was reading the piece instead of playing from memory, my communication with the audience was diminished. This was a fair remark as far as the music itself was concerned. What he could not know was that this concert was the longest interval of our stay in Saigon during which I forgot the differences between myself and the people around me.

The French

More than one hundred years earlier than our arrival, on the eve of the American Civil War, l'Amiral Léonard Victor Joseph Charner entered Saigon with over a thousand men and claimed it for France. The next year Emperor Tu Duc signed a treaty granting France broad political, economic, and religious control of southern Vietnam. By 1890, France had created *l'Indochine*—present-day Vietnam, Cambodia, and Laos—which they relinquished at the Geneva Conference of 1954, after more than ninety years of French development, acculturation, and stemming the nationalist tide. By 1964, Saigon had been ten years under the influence of a new foreign occupation, but the French presence was still evident and pervasive.

The French of Saigon were, in general, crisp and sardonic about how Americans were conducting themselves in Vietnam. During my first month, I attended a ladies luncheon put on by the French cultural mission, hostessed by women who were admirable for their well-cut clothes and hair and sharp remarks. I sensed I was being studied at a glance and dismissed as one more American to be pitied for the naïveté of my understanding of the Vietnamese, including my obvious failure to find the right dressmaker. My defensive reaction to this closed society was dissipated by several unforgettable individuals.

One was a woman who tutored me in French. She came to our house several times a week for three months: a tall, long-necked, stiff-backed blonde of thirty-five, always cool, with white skin, a long, sharp profile, and straight hair piled on top of her head in a stylish modified beehive. She wore elegant silk and cotton sleeveless outfits, high-heeled strap shoes, and spoke in a high, fluty voice. She had been in Saigon for about a year with her husband, who ran a French travel agency. She was a confessed anglophile and very proud of her white skin (she remarked once that she could not bear dark skin), British accent and fluency in English.

She delighted in making assertions about national character based on language. Her lessons were peppered with dicta about the narrow-mindedness of the French compared with the tolerance and earthiness of the English, based on the paucity of French vocabulary for certain expressions that were rendered so colorfully in English. (I was reminded to be vigilant in correcting her *r* in English when it slipped from the British to the French variety.) She saved her heaviest criticism for the Vietnamese, whom she dismissed as "thoroughly unpatriotic."

This precise and prissy manner—which may have been inspired by film versions of the British upper class, since she had never been to England—made her an excellent French tutor. She had an authoritative approach, fast and lively coverage of lessons, and a finickiness about usage and grammar. Criticisms of my pronunciation and usage were sandwiched between bright, amiable compliments about what a gifted student I was (a technique I immediately tried out on a group of Vietnamese students I was tutoring in English).

We invited her and her husband to dinner, where she smiled approvingly at my new smoothness in speaking French. Her husband was smaller and more delicate, in a dark blue business suit and wire-rimmed glasses, with a manner more relaxed, genial, and openly conservative than his wife's.

In our discussions, I was constantly playing a role—the naïve American who needed to have both my French inflections and my perceptions of the world polished to a brighter sheen. For example, one afternoon at our usual place at the dining room table beside the morose potted plants, we discussed the Kennedy assassination at length. She asserted throughout that it was the measure of one's political sophistication whether one realized that the event was the result of a conspiracy rather than the act of one deranged man, as Americans were claiming. At the time, I considered her argument typically European—too subtle, ignorant of the American psyche—but since then have wondered whether subsequent evidence on the event was leaning in her direction.

I was sorry to give up our biweekly sessions when she had to return to France. The French friend who took her place was far too relaxed to do as good a job, and her social duties as the wife of the manager of the Hotel Continental, with two small children, cut short our series of lessons.

The French family running the mountain inn where we stayed in Da Lat had been in Vietnam for four generations. Their Swiss mountain hotel overlooked untilled fields of bright blue, violet, and orange wild flowers and dark green terraced hillsides with scrub bushes and pine in the distance. The family was ruled by a matriarch of about seventy—tall and erect, always dressed in black, with black stockings and dark wool caps. She had dusky, taut skin and a brusque manner. Her son, daughter, and daughter-in-law were gentle people in their thirties, with light curly hair. The only family members untouched by a slight sadness were the son's two children, who carried water buckets and splashed and teased each other along the flagstone paths winding around the inn.

We were the only guests there, since Da Lat was closed off to all but air travel because of the danger of Viet Cong sabotage on the roads. The only time our privacy was broken was the evening two Vietnamese military officers showed up for dinner. At the evening meal, the matriarch would emerge through the swinging door in her dark cap and serve up the delicately buttered vegetables and fruit pies that she herself produced from the inn garden and kitchen. She stood by our table and told her story in severe, economical French. Her father had come to Vietnam in 1900 with the French army. Her brother had opened an iron foundry in Saigon and then lost it paying a friend's debts. The family then had built the present inn, which had supported them comfortably until the French left Vietnam in 1954. Now they were not sure how much longer to keep it open.

The whole family made sure that the fireplaces were lit in the empty rooms, that fresh-cut flowers were placed on the unused tables, and that hot water for baths was available after dinner. Her son was mild-mannered and dreamy. He showed us his insect collection and his library of scientific, philosophic, and Catholic literary works. Her daughter had been to France only once, for a month. She asked wistfully whether we had ever been to Korea and said she wanted to live there and serve, without explaining further.

One evening, we attended the local cinema, also empty, and saw Jean Gabin in *Mélodie en Sous-sol*. Another evening, I read Verne's *Le Tour du Monde en 80 Jours*.

■　■　■

Saigon was a gold mine for journalists and historians who combined long American and Vietnam experience with a native French background. We knew two such men: one a journalist and one a political scientist at an American university. They were similar in the way they talked, with the ironic perspective and sometimes whimsical insights that their long experience in three cultures had provided. The journalist could facilely adapt his language, including his accent, to his audience. One dinner party, he amazed us by speaking French the whole evening with a flat American accent to accommodate both his French-speaking Vietnamese and his American colleagues.

Both of these men were later killed in Vietnam during the same period—the journalist in a military plane crash and the political scientist in the explosion of a land mine on the road to a province north of Saigon. The political scientist gave us a foreshadowing of his last moments when he dryly described his thoughts while once driving with a South Vietnamese army convoy. He saw the car directly ahead of him hit a mine and explode and he remembered thinking at the time, Well, I've had a full life. Vietnam is a big part of it. This is the place for me to go.

■　■　■

Music opened another aspect of French Saigon. I began playing piano trios with two Frenchmen, a cellist and a violinist. The cellist had an extensive library of musical scores, the pages crisscrossed by the wiggly feeding trails of insects, which forced one to improvise abruptly at certain measures. In his fifties, this man was a teacher who had long been with the French cultural mission in Vietnam, where he had raised his family. He had a large, weary, generous face and body and a slight hesitation before speaking, which gave him a thoughtful manner. He showed no interest in political and military events, either in Vietnam or elsewhere, chose to ignore the American presence in Saigon, and never demonstrated any personal attachments to France. He was anxious about his young son, who had diphtheria and whose sad coughing accompanied our playing the one evening we spent at his house.

The violinist was a different type. He was younger, had arrived more recently in Saigon, and had spent years translating Chinese historical novels. He had a thin face, tinted glasses, and a barbed word for everything, including the American role in the war, Saigon life and politics, the French government, and his own performance on the violin. Although less accomplished than the cellist, with an undependable tone, he made up for these deficiencies by vigorously singing along when there were too many notes to handle and dashing through each section with verve and obvious appreciation of the style being called for.

He liked to play with words too, making bad puns in French and challenging me to do the same in English. The bitter edge to his humor might have been due to a tumor, which he referred to vaguely several times as the reason he had to play in an air-conditioned room. He was also worried about his sick child, a few months old and not satisfactorily diagnosed in Saigon, whom his wife was considering taking home to France.

We invited both men and their wives to one of our conglomerate cocktail parties, but the men appeared without their wives and stayed only briefly. They were obviously restless and uncomfortable with the bustling crowd. They both had a strained look on their faces and left quickly, with apologies.

Speaking and Not Speaking French

When surrounded by an all-French conversation, I first understood the special paranoia of feeling lost in a language. My background at the time consisted of several years of high school and one year of college French, the former spent exclusively on writing grammar exercises and the latter on developing a method of reading and writing that could reproduce the gist of a text without revealing a misunderstanding of the details. It was not so difficult to deal with Ba and Chi Hai, whose French was as rudimentary as mine, but dinner-party evenings in French were devastating to my self-esteem. I also concluded—and still think—that there is something inherently antipathetic between me and the French language. A way of pinching the lips together, sending air through the nose, and lifting the ends of sentences that produces a kind of person I am not.

The worst of the French-speaking dinner parties was one given by a world-traveled Vietnamese couple. The husband had been part of the brain trust advising the Diem regime and was serving the same function under the present administration. (He lost a leg during the Tet offensive of 1968.) The most voluble dinner guest that evening was an American academic of great exuberance, with a fund of knowledge on Vietnam. For the sake of two non-English-speaking guests, and for the first time to my ears, he became a Niagara Falls of French, pouring down on all of us, at great speed and with no full stops, his assertions about Vietnam's political dilemma, taking many tortuous paths and byways in making his point.

By the end of the evening, I was in a silent fury, pushed to the brink by the effort of trying both to understand his undoubtedly idiosyncratic French and following the direction of his arguments—all this while surrounded by the other guests, who seemed to have no problem whatsoever in participating and understanding. As we walked home in the dark in a drizzling mist about 11 P.M., my mood was reinforced by the tense streets, which had been cleared by a curfew imposed after a series of student and Buddhist-Catholic rioting.

My language difficulties were complicated further by the fact that we were in a setting seething with confusing syntax and inflections on many levels beyond spoken language. No episode demonstrates this better than the story of my first French tutor. She was a Vietnamese student in her early twenties, born in Hanoi, with a French education. She was a Buddhist, an affiliation that seemed in her case to be more political than religious. Tall and thin, she dressed alternately in a light blue *ao dai* or a skirt and blouse, and had unusually curly short black hair, wide dark eyes, and an intense look of zealotry. Our lessons started with great warmth and enthusiasm as we read *Les Petites Filles Modèles* and she corrected my essays and discussed the French names of Vietnamese fruit and the beauty of Hanoi's changing seasons.

But deterioration set in at a fast rate as her political interests drove us to conversations on the war and the future of Vietnam. She launched into long disquisitions—a snarl of political theory, fervid support for patriotism and the position of Vietnamese dissident Buddhists, and a strong desire to emigrate to the United States. She pronounced the South Vietnamese unpatriotic, especially those who spoke only French, and praised the local Buddhist priests, whom she described cryptically as very knowledgeable about politics but not political. She characterized Buddhism as a liberal religion, superior to Christianity in that regard. She found dictators to be odious, particularly Khanh— whom she felt the Americans were wrong to support because, just like Diem, he did nothing and had no support from "the people." She soured the lunch to which we had invited her by blurting out, on the subject of student rioting: "People say the Americans are starting them to put the Diemists back in power."

Once she wrote out a familiar-looking diagram of her proposed government for Vietnam. There would be a chief of state and three branches, including a legislative assembly, a government "of the people," which she thought could be implemented in one month at most. After lambasting military dictators, she added that there was such a thing as a good dictator, like de Gaulle or Khrushchev, who made the people "very happy." On the other hand, she deplored the Nazi system, which she had seen in films.

From time to time, she referred vaguely to poor health—*mal au foie*—and mentioned wistfully that she could improve with better care in a country like the United States. Our last lesson was a mutual embarrassment. After I had found another, more businesslike tutor, I made the lame excuse that my schedule was too busy. She only looked hurt.

We were to meet once more under the worst of circumstances. In one of our early conversations, she had told me about a benefit for a splinter student party that was forming, and evidently my polite response to her description—a lot of which I did not follow—had given her the erroneous impression I would buy tickets to this affair. About a month after our last lesson, she appeared at our door with tickets and asked for payment. At the time, I thought her tone ugly, but probably she was simply controlling her nerves. Precipitously, I interpreted her coming as an attempt to use our earlier empathy to extort money.

As both our voices got higher and louder, any chance of rational communication became impossible. She left with a red face and a sinister look, mumbling something about American intruders. Behind this misunderstanding over such a trivial matter lay the mutual confusion and frustration of two young women far apart in life experiences who thought they were finding common causes but who were overwhelmed by cross-purposes.

Dinner Dignitaries

Our weekly dinner and cocktail parties now merge into one big event, with voices arguing below the two whirring ceiling fans, Ba moving in and out with attractive dishes and an uneasy smile, resident journalists in their battle fatigues most certain of the facts, visiting American researchers and government officials in short-sleeved shirts asking thoughtful questions and pondering the answers, formally suited Vietnamese civil servants, professors, and former ministers, a few French and British who always seemed to have been around a hundred years longer than the Americans. And there were the women in flowered dresses who were conversing apart, working hard to find common ground with each other, and the rare Vietnamese wife who appeared with her husband. The air was animated, overheated, and claustrophobic.

Several of our Vietnamese guests turned out to be historical figures of some importance. Colonel Pham Nhac Thao, who came several times with his wife, was President Khanh's press secretary at the time and, it later turned out, a Viet Cong secret agent. During that year, he evidently had been involved in a scheme to deseat Khanh and would soon be banished briefly to Washington, out of harm's way. He remains in memory as a watchful man whose savvy manner with foreigners made perfectly believable his life of political machination and intrigue. He was murdered by rivals in the Saigon government and his remains were later transferred by the Communist government to the "patriots' cemetery" near Ho Chi Minh City.

I vaguely remember Madame Thao as thin and anxious and have wondered since how much she knew of her husband's intricate relationships.

Another guest, Dr. Phan Huy Quat, later had occasion to

regret Colonel Thao's mission to stir up trouble in Saigon. In February 1965, a few days after Khanh had appointed Dr. Quat prime minister of a South Vietnamese civilian government, Colonel Thao plotted a coup that led to the ouster of Khanh and four months later of Quat, ushering in the regime of Thieu and Ky.

On the September evening when he dined with us, Dr. Quat was serving as foreign minister in the Khanh government. A physician from North Vietnam with a lifetime of experience in government service, he was a small man with a sculpted head of white hair and a conciliatory manner that made credible his later wide-ranging cabinet appointments. Since he spoke softly at a noisy table and in French, it is the other guests and the atmosphere he set as guest of honor that remain in memory, rather than his words. Three American journalists questioned him eagerly, one, who had just arrived in Saigon, with a cold, even contemptuous manner. Dr. Quat answered all with the same even tones and sad expression.

The party divided into three exclusive groups. One encircled Dr. Quat and the second consisted of two American government officials who showed little interest in him and enjoyed trading insults. USAID official to Asia Foundation representative: "What can you do for me in Saigon?" Asia Foundation representative: "Give you some advice." USAID official: "Nah, I don't get advice—I give it!" The third group consisted of two women, the wife of the Asia Foundation representative and myself. She was painfully thin with a pinched voice that combined oddly with a warm manner and active listening. We both concentrated on the chicken curry, white rice, wine, and crepes, and exchanged stories about being a new American wife in Saigon. Four years later, during the Tet offensive, when the Communists dramatically shifted the war to the urban areas, the Asia Foundation representative lost an eye in a stunning Viet Cong attack on the U.S. Embassy in Saigon.

At one dinner at the Paprika restaurant, two USAID acquaintances introduced us to Bui Diem, at that time editor of the English-language *Saigon Post*. In a characteristic attempt to develop some sophistication about the Saigon scene, I noted in my diary: "Diem very frank, nice, pleasant, sympathetic—but since I've become hardened to politics around here, it's safer to say he's probably a sly, slick, conniving politician underneath." The latter assessment, of course, proved to miss the mark entirely. Diem was appointed aide to Dr. Quat and then became South Vietnam's Ambassador to the United States from 1966–1972, under the Thieu government. He later published a political memoir and is now director of a research institute at an American university.

Tran Van Do, the uncle of Madame Nhu and former foreign minister of South Vietnam under Diem, had served as Vietnamese representative at the 1954 Geneva Conference. At our dinner of six Vietnamese dishes, he talked in slow, dreamy French of how he was stepped on at the conference, not even invited by the Viet Minh and the French to join them in signing the partition of Vietnam into North and South. In a quiet, bitter voice he described the French as the most unjust, making deals with his country after they had already lost it. "They are gamblers who lost the whole place and then offer to sell you the Saigon Cathedral."

He spoke about the then-present American efforts in Vietnam with jaunty words and a defeated tone—a perfect fit with the twelve-year-old black Cadillac convertible he drove to our door, which he was resigned to keeping since no one would buy it.

The British

The British had never ruled Vietnam, but their presence in Southeast Asia for the past two hundred years—particularly in Malaya, Singapore, and Hong Kong, and to a lesser extent in Burma and Thailand—made them resident experts who could still give a word or two of calm advice to the American newcomers.

At a U.S. Embassy dinner party, the guest riveting everyone's attention was the former head of intelligence during the 1960 British war in Malaysia against the Chinese Communist insurgents. Making comparisons to the Americans' task in Vietnam, in terms that we would soon hear repeated often, this Errol Flynn look-alike spoke in strong, flowing paragraphs about how the British won their war: They had deprived the insurgents of their lifeblood by moving the peasants into fortified villages and thus isolating the enemy. Several at the table argued with him that the main difference in the Vietnamese situation was the nature of the enemy. The Viet Cong were not like the Chinese insurgents, an outside guerrilla army easily distinguishable from the peasants, but, rather, inside zealots who were the same people as those we were trying to protect.

The British guest then turned to criticize the U.S. handling of the Saigon political situation, his words echoing through 150 years of British colonial history in India and Asia—about the need for forming good administration and establishing the Rule of Law when building new nations. The Americans at the table shook their heads. We had a different situation in Vietnam.

The differences between French and British styles of colonization became a long-term topic of conversation—particularly the strong cultural infiltration of language, schooling, and intermarriage of the French compared with the dominant administration-building and cultural separation of the British. At the time, I compared the sense of control exuded by British-trained civil servants (like the neat stockinged policemen directing traffic in Singapore) to the disorderly flamboyance of the South Vietnamese military and government officials, which a number of Americans ascribed partly to French influence. The question of whether we Americans should be classed as colonizers and how we compared with our French predecessors was muddled by the ambiguity of our role in Vietnam and the hectic pace of events during those years.

One of the most relaxed households in Saigon was that of an official of the British Advisory Mission. He smoked a pipe and once made the friendly remark that he actually preferred speaking American English because it took so much less trouble to pronounce than British English. We were guests at one of his elegant dinner parties, which was unforgettable for its representativeness. That is, it was clear that each couple was invited as representative of a piece of the Western social fabric of Saigon.

We were the American professor and his young wife. Another guest was a Colonel Blimp type, who was actually a colonel, with a broad mustache, black slicked hair, a bush uniform, long years in Africa and India, and a full repertoire of hilarious stories and an impressive ability to do Churchill imitations. His wife was tall, bony, and long-nosed, with soft white skin outrageously made up. She had a tendency to interject a number of exuberant *Oh really?*s into other people's remarks. A German and a Dutch couple completed the European community. The Dutch couple said very little and the Germans were defenders of Diem.

Our hostess smiled benignly over her sparkling tableware, embroidered linen napkins, uniformed, silent servants, and perfectly cooked roast beef. It is unlikely there was a crystal chandelier in that tropical setting, but my memory has placed one there. Whether or not we discussed the political troubles of Saigon, it is certain that any disagreements or latent hostilities among the guests would have been muted by the genial clinking of silver and our host's generous refilling of the wineglasses at certain points in the conversation. There was nothing extraordinary about this dinner on the standard diplomatic model and I have attended a number since, but this was my first. It remains the epitome of the British colonial ethic, a ritual dinner steeped in gracious, controlled, civilized behavior, holding at bay a world of confusion just outside the door.

Demonstrations

The odd aspect of letters from home was their view that we were living in constant turmoil and danger. Certainly in the Saigon of 1964, there were a large number of political demonstrations against the Khanh government and violent incidents between religious factions, with students the most vocal group. People were killed during riots in the streets, public buildings, and the airport. Students periodically walked around in sullen groups carrying clubs and bricks. Police routed demonstrations by Buddhist monks and nuns. Children were reported injured in a battle between a Buddhist and a Catholic high school. Electricity was shut off periodically during labor strikes. (This prompted one American visitor to assert, "This country is out of order.")

But we ourselves saw no terrorism or violence during our stay, so we relied on the inside information of friends and, like Americans back home, on newspapers—which reached us a few days after the event. The closest we got to active violence was the sunny Sunday morning a week before Thanksgiving when we caught the edge of a tear-gas cloud flowing down our street. It had just been thrown by soldiers in full battle gear, riot helmets, and shields holding at bay a small group of sign carriers come to watch the swearing in of the new civilian government. The gas stung our eyes and throats and forced us inside. Afterward, we went to dinner with an American CIA operative who claimed that Viet Cong agents were behind these demonstrations.

Living in Saigon on a day-to-day schedule cushioned us from feeling threatened by political events. The tendency was to let it all become part of the atmosphere, away from the foreground of our personal lives.

The largest demonstration of that period was one in which we were active observers. One Tuesday morning late in August, as we were having breakfast, we heard loud chanting and ran out the gate to see thousands of students marching down Rue Pasteur to Thong Nhut to call on President Khanh. Walking alongside, we were in a spirited but well-organized crowd of students, professors, and student policemen in orange and yellow arm bands, instructing the marchers when to chant, when to walk, when to sit down.

They were commemorating the anniversary of the death of a Vietnamese girl who had immolated herself the year before, as had over a dozen Buddhist zealots during the Diem regime. This crowd was also going to Khanh to demand that he form a democracy in Vietnam. Specifically, they wanted freedom of press and religion, elimination of the military dictatorship, and the formation of a civilian government with a representative legislature. Even more important than these demands, which would have been impossible to implement in such a weakened structure as that of the Saigon government, was the organized protest itself, demonstrating discontent, a show of people power, and confused nationalist self-assertion and a desire for change.

Several students grabbed our arms and eagerly explained how Americans were wrong to support a "Diemist" like Khanh and that we should be helping the "right" people—none clear on who the right people were. One earnest member of the Faculty of Pedagogy repeated some of the litany: "The grass is still green over Ngo Dinh Diem's grave. . . . Vietnam would be free now if it weren't for foreigners. . . . We are against the military and a dictatorship."

A crowd of 25,000 reached Khanh at the Presidential Palace, where he made the mistake of coming out for verbal jousting with the student leaders. From our viewpoint of thirty yards, he looked small and unimpressive with his sparse goatee as he climbed on a green car to parlay with two students, grabbing one microphone back and forth. In denouncing Khanh as a dictator, one student waved in front of Khanh's nose a copy of the Vung Tau Charter, which Khanh had just promulgated to give himself more authority. (The students later put a match to this copy of the charter.)

Khanh's manner was reluctant and despondent. He stood with stooped shoulders as he shouted incoherent slogans about maintaining the people's freedom and fighting the enemy. The students got more microphone time than he did, and the noise of the swarming crowd and onlookers sitting in trees and on the tops of fences that lined the boulevard blocked out half of the words. Weaponless and bewildered-looking bodyguards and arm-banded student police pushed at the crowd in opposing directions and after ten minutes, Khanh disappeared into the swarming mass and back into the palace.

Rapacious newsmen climbed trees for better views and one with crazy bleached white hair and receding teeth stuck his camera in Khanh's face. We stood beside a gray-hooded Buddhist nun and a novitiate child in the same garb. A young kerchiefed girl with bad teeth felt inexpertly for a pocket to pick along the side of my skirt. I caught her hand and shook my head, partly because the skirt had no pockets.

A sudden violent downpour broke up the crowd, despite the efforts of one student leader who shouted himself hoarse through the bowl of hair over his eyes. The hard rain immediately soaked us all to saturation, so it was useless to seek cover. The crowd, friendly to observers, thought we were especially funny walking home with our clothes plastered to us. One of my students from the school where I was teaching English stepped out of the crowd proudly and said "Hello" and "I'll see you soon"—which may have been all he had learned at that point.

By afternoon, the news was that Khanh had stepped down from his position and that the next day the military council would elect a civil chief of state, would disband the military council and send the generals back to the field, and would arrange for elections of a national assembly.

Khanh was to maintain control of the Saigon government for about six more months. He was then forced to flee the country following the coup plotted by Colonel Thao. (In a 1983 report, Khanh was managing a small restaurant in West Palm Beach, living among old photographs and souvenirs.)

To Americans, this demonstration was one more indication that we were supporting quicksand. (An American acquaintance talked to me about evacuation possibilities at one point.) To Vietnamese, it meant more power struggles, more demonstrations followed by repressions and an increasingly enfeebled Saigon government. At dinner that night, three knowledgeable American friends gave varying perspectives on these demonstrations. One was an anthropologist who had studied the Vietnamese montagnards for over twenty years. He mused about contemporary events in terms of national character, suggesting that the Vietnamese were like the Irish (his own background), suffering from long colonization, with fierce loves and hates, aggressive, childlike, and unpredictable. The second, a CIA agent, was faintly optimistic that the new civilian government would not be as corrupt as the military.

The third, a Defense Department official who had been making dour predictions from the beginning, argued that the U.S. military and Ambassador Taylor were not competent to handle the political tangles. He was convinced that the Buddhist Venerable Tri Quang was pulling the strings in these latest events but would not show his hand publicly. All of these friends asserted that reports from the military on fighting in the countryside were grossly distorted by determined optimism, and the Defense Department official suggested that the return of General Lansdale to Vietnam as adviser in counterinsurgency might bolster the Saigon government.

We walked home that night over deserted streets, fatigued from the tension. The day before, a bomb had been planted in the Eden Theater and killed a man passing by on a motorcycle. The day after, a *plastique* planted on the fifth floor of the Hotel Caravelle wounded five guests. Three days later, during street battles among students and hoodlums using clubs and knives, one fourteen-year-old boy slipped while running away and was hacked to pieces.

Escape

Sleep in Saigon was in equal parts an escape from the heat and escape from tension. It is surprising to count up the hours during the day and night I regularly spent in that other world. Although my daytime dreams have faded from memory, the places they occurred have not: in our air-conditioned bedroom, on top of the green and blue striped bedspread hand-sewn by young girls working in the Indian shop on Catinat; on the cotton twill green and purple flowered cushions of a rattan chair in the office, with a seat so deep and armrests so wide that it was easy to curl up and disappear; on the rattan sofa in the living room, on three cushions of the same cotton twill, under the ceiling fan, my arm dangling a book over the edge, where I would jump up with embarrassment when one of the project staff walked in the front door.

These long and short naps could happen in the late morning or, most often, after lunch and after dinner. Sleep after lunch was often accompanied by the soft thudding of cannon fire miles outside the city. Equally soporific were the heavy rains occurring mostly in the evenings, which blocked out all other sounds and sent a cool perfumed mist through the windows.

In the late afternoon and evening, I also read, slowly and thoroughly, making exotic choices as far away as imaginable from what we were seeing and reading about Saigon in *The New York Times* and *Newsweek*: Oscar Lewis's *Children of Sanchez, Miss Julie,* Verne's *Le Tour du Monde en 80 Jours,* discovering it to be a satire. *The Magic Mountain* was a faraway country, obtained from the British Council Library and not available at the German Cultural Center. I noted cryptically in the margin that I was becoming an anglophile. *The Tin Drum* suited particularly well because of its bizarre and bitter humor. *Buddenbrooks* was a long, slow read, the final page reached with regret. Following an impulse for self-improvement, I started Maurois's *L'Histoire des Etats-Unis* but have no memory of its contents. Daudet's *Lettres de Mon Moulin,* a gift from my French tutor, came at the end of our stay, when it was too quiet a book to compete with our wrapping-up activities.

I have never since listened to the radio with the regularity and pleasure I did in Saigon. On a day I spent sleeping off a bout of mild dysentery, a large twenty-six-inch Grundig arrived from Hong Kong. I spent many evenings after that eagerly pressing buttons and turning the heavy dial, watching the bright green lines dart across Moscow and Paris and London. There was a surprising availability of accessories and antennae in the Saigon shops I visited, where the owners were eager to discuss matters of equipment and reception and advise me on how to make contact with remote distances.

Since the proper antenna for our model was not available, however, I relied on the splendid BBC for news, then switched to distant numbers at the other end of the dial for the exotic, urgent sounds of Russian and Chinese coming in through the static like pilots about to be shot down, popular Vietnamese songstresses wailing romantically and permanently off key, and Western classical and popular music from Hong Kong and the U.S. military station. One evening, I caught the full original sound track of Kurt Weill's *Lady in the Dark.* The poignancy and straining melodies sank deeply. The leaping notes of "My Ship Has Sails" still burst into my mind from time to time, even though all but the first four words have disappeared.

Side Trips

One way to understand the special character of Saigon was to leave it for a while. Even the leaving was negotiated tensely, with aggravation. When we purchased the Air Vietnam tickets for our September weekend in the mountains of Da Lat, the women behind the counter were deliberately cool, slow, not making eye contact and answering questions with a minimal, ambiguous nod. This never inspired confidence that arrangements were confirmed or even fully understood. But like emigrating birds, we finally rose up and over the mountains to sunny cool weather of seventy degrees.

The terraced hillsides, wild flowers, audible bird population, and stillness in the air provided the needed refreshment—although the stillness soon took on a disturbing aspect. During that first afternoon, when we bought red and black Cham rugs and spent the evening at a French film, we seemed to be the only customers; the woman selling us the rugs did not even haggle over our offer. At the mountain inn where we were the only guests, the French family running the place told us their history with a melancholy air.

The security precautions that limited access to Da Lat took on a reality when our return to Saigon was delayed by the mini coup staged by Generals Lam Van Phat and Duong Van Duc. To fill out the extra day—while the coup collapsed in twenty-four hours—we toured the nightmare home of Madame Nhu, sister-in-law of President Ngo Dinh Diem and the "Dragon Lady" of his regime. With embarrassment and neglect, the Saigon government maintained her home as a museum. The house was bizarre and demented, a pink cement and wood structure, all doorways, hallways, and sharp, meaningless turns, with almost no natural light allowed in at any point. American fixtures were evident everywhere, many of them affixed in places for which they had never been intended, like the fully equipped barber chair screwed to the floor of a bedroom or the large white cabinet with narrow drawers that usually housed hypodermic needles in a doctor's examining room.

The jumble of furniture, equipment, and personal touches—the moldy stuffed animal heads sitting on odd pieces of furniture—loomed out of the dark corners and cast a sinister air over all, feeding the imagination as to the real purposes for such alien furnishings. A garden of weeds and dead grass was dominated by a cement path that spread out in five directions at once, a replica, we were told, of Madame Nhu's hand. This encircled an irregular pond that was purported to be the shape of Vietnam.

Da Lat was still Vietnam. Singapore, however, was not. Singapore was a shining white city with glistening high buildings and a bustle of people emitting rays of high energy—policemen with knee socks and swagger sticks conducting the raucous symphony of cars, trucks, and pushcarts; Chinese, Japanese, Indians, and Malays distinguishable from each other; streets lined with food stalls selling noodles and roasted meat and mountains of fruit undulating under striped canopies.

We stayed with friends in their neat house not far from a British golf and tennis club that had grass courts and older women in saris retrieving the balls with great dignity. In front of our friends' house, Tamil children with delicate features and skin of gleaming ebony flew kites made of colored paper and cloth. The climax of their play was when one of these homemade birds cut loose from its master's hand and swept in zigzag patterns through the eucalyptus trees higher and higher in the bright blue air, and finally disappearing against the clouds.

Late one evening, we walked behind the back row of a crowd of people, mostly children, sitting on the grass, enraptured by a six-hour Indian film—an interminable saga of suffering and love and small triumphs. We visited Nanying University and had dinner with Japanese, British, and Chinese colleagues of our host.

Most amazing were the undeveloped wide spaces outside

the city—miles of white, unoccupied beaches along the South China Sea, which were lined in the distance with thick jungle or the unequivocally straight lines of rubber trees slowly dripping sap into waiting cups. We passed equally neat lines of school-children in long white smocks and green underskirts, the Indian boys with hair tightly wound in topknots. An Australian jungle-warfare training group hunched across the highway in single file and into the underbrush, their camouflage uniforms and polished rifles much too starched and bright to be mistaken for ferns and sunlight. Our final evening, after dinner at a cavernous Chinese restaurant where we were the only couples dancing to the vaguely familiar American music being produced by an eight-piece band, we drove to the top of Mt. Nabor and stared at the harbor lights.

Cambodia was a trip into the past of Southeast Asia, both its recent colonial past and the greater grandeur of the Khmer empire. Cambodia was showing signs of strain that year. Despite Prince Sihanouk's foxy efforts to keep his country neutral in the neighboring war, he was at the time moving away from United States protection and toward China, and was permitting the Viet-namese Communists to set up bases in Cambodia, calculating that they would be the eventual winners. The weekend in mid-November that we flew to Phnom Penh, American dependents were being evacuated and the USIS library had just been sacked.

Invaded over and over by its large and small neighbors during the past six hundred years, Cambodia had its own proud period of dominance when the Khmer empire of the twelfth century stretched from the South China Sea, including parts of central Vietnam, into Burma. It was the grand temples of this period that we visited, with their tributes to Buddha, Hindu legends, and the god-king rulers who built them. Cambodia had a heavier imprint of Indian culture than did Vietnam, apparent in its language, religion, arts, and especially in these temples. Three years before Sihanouk invited Jackie Kennedy to the Angkor temples to improve his relations with the Americans, we toured Angkor Wat, Angkor Thom, and Ta Prohm.

In late afternoon, we slowly walked the mile from one of the four high-roofed, arched entryways, under a canopy of thousands of nesting bats, along the wide stone road to the central edifice of stepped rectangular stone buildings that made up the temple-tomb of Angkor Wat. In the golden light of sunset and deep shadows, each level merged with the next into a panorama of life, bursting with god, human, and animal figures carved in relief, mixing history, myth, and religious belief.

Marching in a long, formal procession of an ancient Khmer king, complete with Indian fan-shaped instruments and favorite pieces of the deceased's furniture, are grinning monkey men with dancing limbs and ornate skullcaps. Balanced on one foot on the tip of an accurately carved lotus blossom is a half-man/half woman angel with arms and one leg raised in praise of creation, in the pose of the classical Cambodian dance. Peasants squat before fish traps next to battles between huge snakes and lion-headed monsters whose devouring of each other gets lost in the abstract, symmetrical swirl of limbs, tails, and teeth. The climb to the highest level of the inner temple displays a panorama of perfect squared symmetry, the same as one sees from the entranceway, or by air. On our walk back, white spotlights turned the great stone blocks of the temple-tomb to carved ivory.

Angkor Thom is pervaded by the person of the Khmer king who built it. His gigantic stone head with half-closed eyes and condescending smile looms over each of the four gates. At these entryways, variations of that face are repeated in the long rows of giants holding a snake on their knees. They have feet larger than their faces and expressions either of benevolence or evil intent. The carvings on the inside walls focus on the common life, with people in the same postures engaging in the same activities with the same tools as those still in the villages outside the temple walls.

Ta Prohm was an important antidote to the glorification of humanity displayed by the other two temples. Here the jungle had been allowed to take over and the voracious tree roots, many of them several yards thick, were snaking over and through the stones, tearing them from their moorings and slowly strangling the whole monument. The result was a green beauty of an age much older than the monument's. The temple was now primordial, with impenetrable overgrowth promising to bury the whole in one hundred more years. Because our motor-powered cyclo had broken down, we sat for an hour on the shaded mossy stones at the edge of the temple. A few children with soft, shy voices offered to sell a few trinkets and then sat with us, smiling a little at our questions and watching our faces.

Contemporary Cambodia was dressing up for the Fête des Eaux. In Phnom Penh, the most stunning aspect of the buildings were the roofs, with elongated sharp corners like bird beaks curved upward and like the long fingers of classical Cambodian dancers. The buildings had just been painted bright red and yellow and pink, in commemoration of the tenth anniversary of independence from French rule. Prince Sihanouk's fairy-tale palace was filled with extravagantly gold-gilded furniture, walls, and mirrors and a throne under a filigreed umbrella with woven gold tassels. The long series of white steps at the palace entrance was flanked by simply carved gold and white lions and griffins.

People in the streets were unconcerned about our presence, glancing idly at us for a moment only. It gave us the pleasure of feeling like tourists, completely temporary rather than interlopers in the rhythm of their lives. That night, without having to buy tickets, we took a front-row seat at a musical show put on by a visiting dance troupe from North Vietnam. We were delighted at getting a glimpse behind our enemy's lines and at noticing that we were the only Westerners in the audience.

Although word seemed not to have filtered down to the street level, official Phnom Penh was not looking favorably on Americans at that time. Our hostess, a public-affairs officer in the U.S. Embassy, lived comfortably in a large mission house with white columns but was disgruntled and frustrated because Sihanouk had just cut off contact between her and her Cambodian counterparts. She had to rely on foreign journalists and varieties of American and European expatriates for word about events inside the country.

Expatriates in such a traditional setting often take on a bizarre tinge. One evening at a café, our hostess pointed out a woman with dyed hair who was dressed in tight silk and feathers and had an extremely edgy manner. She was speaking French with an unrecognizable accent but identified herself as French, or more vaguely, the widow of a French army officer. She claimed to have been Sihanouk's mistress and was rumored to be a native of either Brooklyn or Chicago.

There were two other reminders of the American presence in Cambodia. One was the strange sight of a wrecked American military transport plane on display on the main street, supposedly shot down by Cambodian antiaircraft guns over Cambodian territory. The boarded-up windows and hostile-looking graffiti on the front of the small USIS library, permanently closed, were the second reminder.

At the time, however, these were only curiosities. They were easily passed over for the slow, traditional pace of life that murmured in our ears like the warble of the Cambodian r spoken by our cyclo driver as he pedaled us along a cool street on our last night in Phnom Penh.

Viet Cong Motivation and Morale

A minister under South Vietnamese President Ngo Dinh Diem was the first to apply the term *Viet Cong*, Vietnamese Communist, to the Vietnamese revolutionaries, in order to cast opprobrium on their movement. The Americans retained the term, following the lead of the British in the Malaysian war of 1960, when they labeled the Chinese insurgents CTs, for Communist Terrorists. In 1964, both South Vietnamese and American officials seemed to believe that the Viet Cong were an ill-disciplined band of terrorists and kidnappers of young boys whose hit-and-run tactics had no appeal to the peasantry. A common saying among the Saigon bourgeoisie about the peasants was: *Il ne veut que son petit lopin de terre et qu'on lui fiche la paix.* (He just wants his little plot of land and to be left in peace.)

The goal of the RAND corporation project that took us to Saigon was to develop a realistic picture of the Viet Cong, particularly the motivation behind the movement. The research team consisted of two American directors and about twenty Vietnamese interviewers, plus a staff of Vietnamese and Americans who typed, translated, and compiled the interview material. All these people moved constantly in and out of our house, most of which had been converted to suites of offices.

The team developed a set of interviews never before collected—of Viet Cong prisoners and defectors—that gave a disconcerting picture of the Communist movement. They found that the Viet Cong were formidable—a highly politicized and well-organized group who had seized the nationalist cause and were successful in recruiting and propagandizing among the peasantry. A State Department official later commented that these interview data were like the first reports of the structure and motivation of the Chinese Communist movement that came out in the 1940s.

The project team traveled throughout South Vietnam to get samples of different areas and layers of the Communist movement. There were the southern Viet Minh soldiers who were sent to the North after the 1954 Geneva Conference and, beginning in late 1959, were infiltrated back south through the Ho Chi Minh Trail; there were those cadres who stayed in the South after 1954 and the new members whom they recruited; and there were ethnic Northerners who by 1964 were ordered to the South to prepare for the "general uprising."

Upon completion of their study in Saigon in December 1964, the American directors of the project briefed General Westmoreland, the U.S. Embassy country team headed by Ambassador Taylor, and Vietnamese officials. When they returned to Washington, they briefed Assistant Secretary of Defense McNaughton and the Head of the Vietnam Working Group at the State Department.

Their conclusions paralleled the CIA assessment at the end of 1964—as revealed in *The Pentagon Papers*: that the Communists were getting stronger and the Saigon side getting weaker. The CIA advised that if current trends were to continue and there were no significant increases in U.S. forces, the Communists might win in 1965.

The revolutionary attitude of the Viet Cong interviewees from the project was summed up by this Southern cadre who was captured in May 1964:

> From 1957 to 1960 the cadres who had remained in the South had almost all been arrested. Only one or two cadres were left for every four or five villages. What was amazing was how these one or two cadres started the movement so well. If at that time the government in the South had been a good one, if it had not been dictatorial, if the agrarian reforms had worked, if it had established control at the village

level, then launching the movement would have been difficult. We succeeded, not because these cadres were exceptionally gifted but because the people were ready for rebellion. The people were like a mound of straw, ready to be ignited.

The Vietnamese Team

The Vietnamese interviewers for the project, who were members of the Saigon bourgeoisie, were shaken by the zeal with which their interviewees repeated the Communist doctrine of ridding the country of foreigners and corrupt puppet governments. Several of the interviewers for the project were Vietnamese professors from the National Institute of Administration and from the Faculty of Law, University of Saigon. One in particular always had witty words and a weary expression that indicated he had none of the official rosy optimism about the future of South Vietnam. Embarrassed by his English, he spoke only in eloquent French with a slightly bitter taste, asking probing questions of the Americans he met and then keeping his own counsel. He was not able to leave after the Communist takeover, whether out of patriotism or torpidity, and emigrated to Australia in the early 1980s after suffering the loss of his position and hardship to his family.

Another, who directed research on Vietnamese foreign relations, was the philosopher, even the mystic, of the Vietnamese team. His interviews for the project were sensitive and perceptive, and, judging by his devotion to the work, he must have felt he was finding out something about his compatriots that would make a difference in the course of the war. His manner was invariably gentle even when his sensibilities were bruised, as they often were by the brusque manners of some American visitors and colleagues. His story turned stranger after he emigrated to the United States in 1975 and found it impossible to become a capitalistic entrepreneur. After having trouble getting a job in Washington, he moved to Houston, where he wrote us strange letters about Buddhism and sense of self.

Much more practical was a former University of Saigon student who taught social science at a Buddhist university at the time of the project. He had studied in the United States and was struggling mightily through his political-science background to find a political solution to the war. Throughout breakfast with us one morning, he spoke in a tense semiwhisper about his latest theory: The United States should fuel the Sino-Soviet split by increasing hostilities toward the U.S.S.R. and opening relations with China, thereby cutting off China as a source of supply for the North Vietnamese, thereby isolating the Soviets and the North, thereby forcing the North to negotiate with the South on equal terms. He felt certain that neutralism and a coalition government in Vietnam were inevitable, and that the United States and Saigon should stop wasting lives and start preparing a government that could formally recognize the Communists without being overrun by them. He considered Khanh "a boy, not a boss." At the time, most of these solutions of his were greeted with polite skepticism, given the Americans' commitment to winning the war.

One evening, he and several friends took us outside Saigon to a restaurant along a stream, where we sat in the dark under the trees, on a long wooden porch, eating shrimp and cooked vegetables and laughing at stories of their student days at the University of Saigon in 1960. Another evening, he invited us to a Chinese restaurant with his fiancée, prospective father-in-law, and uncle, all of whom explained how they were waiting until the stars moved into a propitious position to set the marriage date.

After the Communist takeover, he stayed in Vietnam, apparently because departure arrangements fell through. For some years, he just survived with no position, while his wife painted Impressionist-style portraits that they sold to people who were emigrating. He was eventually hired by the University of Saigon to teach English. In the early 1980s, he emigrated with his family to the Boston area, where his sons are attending college—one a musician and the other a tennis player. He works for a state social-service agency dealing with refugee resettlement.

Of the three Vietnamese women who staffed the project, two always wore the traditional *ao dai,* and the third, the youngest, wore tight short skirts and high heels favored by the French. All, unmarried, devoted themselves full time to their jobs. The oldest, who had spent nine years in the United States, where she studied at a university, was desperately searching for the right niche in the crumbling social milieu of Saigon. She was invariably soft-spoken and open and plain in manner, her pained expression broken only when she could actually help by recommending an American-trained dentist or arbitrating disputes between Ba and Chi Hai. Years later, we saw a piece by her in the *Washington Post.* Her colleague who also wore traditional dress, who was a devout Catholic, had one brother serving as a priest in Vietnam and another was a professor at an American university.

Every morning at 8:30, the youngest staff member clicked through our front door and up the stairs to the office with a brilliant smile and black spike heels that left permanent traces in our memories if not on the hard tile floors. She was fondly referred to as Betty Boop by some of the American team and it became difficult to conceive of starting the workday without her rousing entrance.

Uniforms

Returning to Saigon from Da Lat, we waited in the Da Lat airport with a U.S. Marine captain, as Saigon straightened out its air schedule in the aftermath of the failed twenty-four-hour coup. This marine was every inch a professional soldier, cropped brown hair and light blue eyes squinting with determination as he described the military picture as he saw it. His major frustration was that the South Vietnamese soldiers (whom he reidentified as simply "the Vietnamese") had no ambition, grit, or organization with which to fight this war. Continually pushing the long sleeves of his uniform above his elbows while sitting upright on a wooden bench, he described the Vietnamese as self-protective and fragmented, uneager to learn how to use their weapons and undergo combat training, poker-faced when harangued by their own officers—who themselves limited their energies to furthering their own careers and to demanding American heavy weaponry to shield them from taking casualties.

Since the first American combat troops did not arrive in Vietnam until six months later, this marine captain was still in the advisory capacity begun ten years earlier when the United States agreed to train the South Vietnamese army after the 1954 Geneva Accords. But it was clear during that two-hour conversation in Da Lat that being an adviser was not enough for him and hundreds of others he must have represented. He saw a cleanup job to be done that he was certain Americans could accomplish in a year or less if allowed to do it themselves.

He was untroubled by the thrashing around of the Saigon government, which, like the poor troop morale, he interpreted as one more indication of flawed national character. Local politics was messy and irrelevant to the enterprise for which he had been trained. It was clearly his war now, not theirs. When asked whether the enemy suggested a different picture of Vietnamese morale and national character, he shook his head and laughed, saying, "They're not so tough. Just let us at them." As we boarded the plane together, he gave me a delicately carved montagnard bracelet.

At the time, I was impressed by the captain. A man in uniform among civilians assumes the power of the supernatural: He symbolizes other realms we never enter, hard realities we could not possibly comprehend, and he takes on the mystery that comes from serving others by offering to lose oneself. In the Saigon of 1964, it was still possible to feel this way about a uniform, while American soldiers still moved robust and handsome through the streets, before the bloody ugliness and the futility of counting bodies in an endless guerrilla war took over our consciousness completely and removed the shine forever.

The uniform worked its powers on Americans and Vietnamese alike. One morning, a shiny jeep rolled up our driveway and a splendidly pressed and ribboned South Vietnamese army officer in new black combat boots leaped out onto the red tiles of our front veranda. His smile was brilliant, radiating energy, and it took me a few minutes to realize that this was the slight, deferential former student in soft white shirts and scuffed shoes who had been working on the project the week before. We had no further word about him after he left Saigon for his assignment, but I prefer to think of him as fixed permanently and glowing on our front veranda.

Xenophobia

Hue was the ancient imperial capital of Vietnam, where the Gia Long dynasty began in 1802 and ended in 1954 with Bao Dai as the last emperor. Emperor Gia Long and his successor, Minh Mang, in order to rebuff European attempts to spread influence in Asia, adopted an isolationism on the Chinese model. Hue was built as a walled city, like Beijing, and its rulers established a Confucian administration, a highly structured and static hierarchy that did not tolerate innovation or Western barbarians. (When the first American, Captain John White of Salem, sailed into Saigon harbor in 1820, he was spurned, as had been his European predecessors.)

Hue, in the center of Vietnam near the 17th Parallel, has endured as a seedbed of Vietnamese nationalism and violent revolution against foreign domination. Ho Chi Minh's father became an official in the imperial court at Hue and the young Ho attended a French school there within a climate of dissidence and political turmoil. Ngo Dinh Diem, an ardent nationalist whose fate took a different path, was born in Hue and attended school there, where his father was also a member of the imperial court. Vo Nguyen Giap, Vietnam's most brilliant military commander, was born of a peasant father in central Vietnam and attended the private school in Hue run by Ngo Dinh Diem's father, where nationalist ideology pervaded the curriculum.

Hue was the site of two of the most bitter conflagrations of the Vietnam War since the French defeat of 1954. During the massive Tet offensive of January 1968, when the Communists besieged all U.S. and South Vietnamese strongholds simultaneously, the battle for Hue was the worst bloodbath of the whole war, with unprecedented atrocities committed by the Communists in the twenty-five days they held the city.

The second event was earlier, with a different political basis. The Buddhists of Vietnam, political activists throughout Vietnam's recent history, were always considered a dissident group, first by the Confucian emperors and then by the Catholic-dominated regimes of the French and Ngo Dinh Diem. In May 1963, the Buddhists had centered their appeal for national cohesion in Hue, where several thousand gathered to celebrate Buddha's birthday and hear speeches. The Catholic mayor ordered five armored cars to disperse the crowd, resulting in one woman and eight children being killed. Well-organized Buddhist protests and agitation in the next few weeks were followed by more brutal repression by the Diem regime. The climax of the Hue massacre occurred in June 1963 when the first Buddhist monk immolated himself on a Saigon street in protest against the Diem government.

A little over a year later, we went to Hue for two days. We were invited by a poetic German doctor teaching at a medical school there. He had become enthralled with traditional Vietnam and wanted to show us the beauty of Hue's temples and palaces. But I have no memory of having seen them on that trip.

Our small plane landed in the Hue airport with everyone on board sick from a lurching ride, except for two Indian soldiers from the International Control Commission on whose jaunty uniforms and animated conversation I focused in order to take my mind off a creeping nausea. Our host took us to a deserted Cercle Sportif veranda for lunch and then to his small house to nap under mosquito netting in the intense heat of early afternoon. At about three o'clock, we set out for a walk around the city.

As the three of us ambled along a dirt road beside a narrow, muddy river with green branches and grass bending over it, our host making occasional remarks in soft tones, a silence and stillness began to dominate the scene. A few people and vehicles moved about slowly here and there on the streets, and no Westerners were visible other than ourselves. After about fifteen minutes, we began to draw a small crowd of children unlike any I have ever encountered before or since.

They were sturdy and silent at first, some in old cotton shirts and pants and others in nothing at all, perched on their older sisters' hips. It was their expressions that were arresting— they kept pace with us, first behind and then beside, and watched our faces with grim, old people's eyes, despite the fact that some of them were grinning. As the pack grew, I became the focus of their attention. Some began hooting "Mee [American] . . . Hello . . . Okay" in tones no way like the jaunty and sometimes beseeching children of Saigon, and some kicked rocks at my feet. A few became bolder and, with that same terrible grin, knocked into me, touching my bare upper arms and clothing, while others started throwing pebbles at my back and legs. Then, around the edges of the crowd, their parents started to follow, with somber faces and folded arms, watching intently but making no move to call the children off.

My own reaction was astounding. A rage rose in my throat. I shouted at the nearest and even pushed to the ground one girl of about five who had grabbed on to the back of my skirt. This brought on more hooting from the children, more grim nods from the parents, and a sudden murderous vision to my mind of driving the whole crowd into the muddy river with fire hoses. My two companions advised that I should act unconcerned, and our host tried ordering them away in Vietnamese. We finally were forced to flag a *cyclopousse* and return home.

None of the rest of our visit remains in my memory. Years later, there was a report that after the Tet offensive, the bodies of a German doctor and his wife, and two German colleagues teaching at the medical school in Hue, were found in a shallow pit.

I have never been able to fully account for the hatred aroused in me by this experience. Our host took a psychological view, explaining that because Hue was a tradition-bound city and fiercely nationalistic, foreigners were a threat and had to be considered not only alien but less than human. I was, therefore, a foreign object, something to experiment with, outside the normal protocol of social behavior. In addition, a Western woman walking in the street was a rare occurrence, making me even more of a curiosity. This would explain my outrage—the devastating feeling of being treated like a mad dog, particularly by young children toward whom the normal instinct is to be protective.

But there was more to this than my own personal reaction. There had been past occasions in Saigon when we had also provoked laughter and finger pointing among a crowd of Vietnamese. There was the afternoon we tried to ride double on a flimsy Saigon bicycle and bent the poor vehicle in two while turning at a busy corner. This produced loud giggles from spectators, whom we joined in laughing. Also, for some reason, the sight of Americans caught in a heavy rain was a reason for merriment. On two occasions, we walked home from demonstrations in a downpour, with our clothes and hair plastered to our backs, and were untroubled by the smiles and pointing of other pedestrians who were in exactly the same state.

Then there was the time I took a taxi to the Chinese section of Saigon to investigate a piano factory and hurried back into the cab in confusion upon finding an establishment far too primitive for my needs. A group of children on the sidewalk knocked on the taxi windows and even reopened the door as the taxi pulled away. They shouted something in a singsong taunt before the old man building the pianos ordered them back into the shop. My startled, finicky manner seemed an appropriate thing to laugh at and I waved at them through the back window.

In all these Saigon incidents, the effect on us was benign. Saigon still had a befuddled graciousness, something like the aging ladies of Tennessee Williams who invent their own salvation by courting outsiders with whom they try to maintain a romance about their pasts. In Saigon, we participated in that world with the Vietnamese out of mutual need; their natural hostility to a foreign presence was muted, ubiquitous but disguised, made ambiguous by the history of the city that seeped up through the sidewalks of Rue Catinat and the elegant French-built buildings and schools and the bright new army and roads contributed by the Americans. Saigon had for a very long time spoken Vietnamese with a foreign accent.

The older, deeper Vietnam rose up in Hue and struck us across the face. As her would-be protectors, we had no alternative but to get out.

■　　■　　■

The Hue incident occurred in October, two months before we left Saigon, but it reappeared on our last day, at the airport. The entire project staff and other friends had come, giving us farewell gifts and warm personal remarks. Our photographs show that everyone was smiling, but I remember that their eyes were somber and anxious. Samuel Johnson once said that we will always feel a kind of sorrow at our last moment in a place, no matter how we may have felt about the experience, because "the last" means irrevocable change, a kind of death to the people and place and the piece of ourselves we leave behind.

But this probably described my thoughts more than those of our Saigon friends. Our departure forced them to more practical concerns, to make new plans for a future that loomed gray and unstable. As for me, shaking the hands of Chi Hai and Ba and Chi Bai and thinking about the Saigon-made tweed suits and Thai silk dress in our suitcases and the paintings and cloth and Cambodian rubbings being shipped home cast a reassuring warmth and feeling of permanence over the occasion.

How much more startling, then, was my reaction in the next half hour after the party had left, when we awaited a delayed plane and I glanced idly at the strangers sitting around us—some peasants with bundled straw baskets and food boxes and sleeping babies, some soldiers restlessly smoking and pacing, some fashionably dressed families dealing with travel agents with restrained impatience. As I looked around, a powerful revulsion for every person in the place suddenly struck, one big blind prejudice against the whole people, the whole room, the whole country. It was inexplicable after the warm regret experienced thirty minutes before, and drove me to the exit gate, eager to escape this dark presence.

At the time and later, I could find no events in my own

experience to explain such a reaction, unless it was something about Hue, still festering in a dark corner of the mind.

Those around us were unaware and unconcerned. The official in military uniform handed back our papers with a curt nod, unlocked the high chain-link fence that was the departure gate, hurried us through, and shut it behind us with a clang.

Afterword

I dreamed we were in Saigon again, in our big house with the cavernous spaces and whirring fans and sunlight streaming through the windows, casting long barred shadows across the tile floor. Crowds of busy people nodded politely as they moved in and out of the front door.

My chest was tight with fear for them and I kept trying to call out and get to the front door to prevent them from leaving, but I could not speak and could not move.

Then I turned around and we were standing in the sunny kitchen of our New England summer home of 1983, talking to the Vietnamese friend we knew the best, the former student who during a Saigon breakfast had pressed upon us so earnestly his political solution for neutralization and a coalition government. He had actually visited us in New England during the summer of 1983 and looked in the dream as he had then—little changed, his black hair turned gray, his face a little fuller and more fatigued, his speech coming in uncomfortable bursts of not-quite-correct and highly abstract English.

With the familiar soft voice and vague smile, he answered my polite questions about his wife and children but kept averting his eyes and turning his head away. I was overcome with remorse and wanted to know what he was thinking, but was afraid to ask. I turned away also.

Yet I awoke with a vague sense of gratitude, and the lingering impression that it was actually Saigon where he had come back to see us, and that he was still there, smiling at us a little.

Searching for Vientiane

Vientiane never took hold in my mind as a city of marked character. Part of the reason may have been that in 1967, in contrast to our stay in Saigon three years earlier, I was seeing Laos as a professional. I was assisting on a study of the Lao Communist movement, the Pathet Lao, which eight years after our visit took over the country and began a new kind of nation building. The project involved extensive interviewing of Pathet Lao prisoners and defectors, which meant working part of the time in semisecret.

This secrecy reflected the nature of U.S. involvement in Laos during that period. United States funding and advisers were shoring up the Royal Lao Government against a growing Lao Communist consolidation of the eastern areas of the country. More quietly, the United States concentrated on arming the Hmong tribes of the region, whose historical impulse to remain autonomous and reputation as fierce fighters made them a convenient bulwark against the Communists. Through the course of the war in Laos, nearly seventy thousand Hmong were evacuated from their homelands west to the rim of the Plain of Jars. They left their homes without a harvest crop and with few belongings, supplied solely by USAID and the CIA through its airline, Air America. (By the end of the war in Laos in 1975, the Hmong had lost a high percentage of their male population above the age of thirteen, despite U.S./CIA efforts to build up their forces and resettle their people.)

Another primary reason for U.S. concern was that North Vietnam was using northern and eastern Laos to infiltrate troops into southern Vietnam. It was in order to destroy this infiltration route and prevent North Vietnamese incursions into Laos that the U.S. began an unpublicized bombing of Laos in October

1964. By 1968, a few months after we had left Vientiane, President Johnson had begun a bombardment of eastern Laos that doubled the 1967 bombing of the area and sent into the Royal Lao Government zone a flood of refugees, organized into resettlement centers supported by U.S. aid. Because U.S. actions, like those of the North Vietnamese, were violating the Geneva Accords of 1962 that maintained the neutrality of Laos, our role in the country was kept fuzzy in the public mind—which included my own understanding at the time.

But it was not just our unclear commitment to Laos and the Royal Lao Government that made Vientiane remote for me. Throughout its entire history and prehistory, Laos was a crossing place for many peoples and more powerful neighbors, in conquest or flight, so that ruling governments at any one time had to learn accommodation. The present borders of the country, as defined by the French, do not accurately circumscribe the Lao people, since eastern Thailand holds more lowland Lao than does Laos itself, while the mountain people of northeastern Laos are more heavily represented across the border in Vietnam.

Such a history must create in a small, backward country like Laos, with no access to the sea and a sparse, disparate population, an inherent elusiveness especially remarkable in an age of national self-assertion. When I look at the map of Laos, I always see the shape of an old fashioned spinster with topknot and high-necked dress, her long sharp nose and receding chin bowing politely toward Thailand, Burma, and India, her back and neck bending gracefully under China and Vietnam—and Vientiane at the edge of her lips. I would like to have known her better.

Cycling

Except for the few major roads paved by the French and Americans, the streets of Vientiane were dusty red clay. We traveled everywhere on the green Thai bicycles we bought the week of our arrival, with wicker baskets attached by leather straps to the handlebars, and headlamps that jiggled and flickered on evening excursions. Evenings were the best times to ride, bumping over the cement squares and past the low white wall and twin pillars of our driveway, onto a soft one-lane road. This road, alongside a rice paddy, was new, to provide access to the four concrete ranch-style houses built for foreigners to buy or rent. The other three families on that road were a French couple in private business who owned several cats, an American USAID family with two young children who became our closest friends, and directly across from us, an Indian family with a newborn and a pair of fierce white geese who attacked all intruders whether snakes or people and honked intermittently throughout the day.

Rolling along silently in the dark and sending out clouds of dust, we turned abruptly right to join That Luang, the main road toward town, passing a dark buffalo shape and a few wooden huts on stilts. Lanterns on the huts threw light on peoples' faces and on the long skirts and thonged feet of people cooking meals and shaking out woven cloths. Their voices, especially those of the childrens, carried across the moist air rising from the paddies on either side of us.

We hiked our front wheels onto the rough blacktop of That Luang road, named for the stupa at one end built in 1566 by King Settathirath, the founder of Vientiane. At one time, the stupa enshrined the Emerald Buddha, until it was taken as booty by the Siamese in the nineteenth century. Pedaling in the opposite direction took us to Vientiane's centerpiece, a large monument honoring those killed in war, built by a general in imitation of the French Arc de Triomphe. It stood sixty feet high astride Lan Xang Avenue, looming in the dark like a huge elephant dressed in Hindu finery permanently ready for a parade. At night, we passed ox carts, other bicycles, and a few small cars. I liked to ride single file and second in line in order to get advance notice on sudden appearances of buffaloes or approaching bicycles or cars without lights—but most of the time we rode in blue-black silence.

A left turn at the monument took us through the empty morning marketplace, with woven baskets and plastic bags sitting in silent clumps, across three royally named streets—Sam Sen Thai, Settha Thirath, and finally Fa Ngoun, the king who founded this Kingdom of the Million Elephants—to the Mekong River and the lights of Thailand across its banks. This mighty River of the Nine Dragons rises high in the Asian heartland and flows 1,100 miles through Tibet and China, then another 1,500 miles through Southeast Asia, pouring its nine tributaries through the delta of southern Vietnam into the South China Sea.

When we first arrived in Vientiane in January 1967, we could have walked across the Mekong, only a damp sandbar, but by late summer, it flowed and gleamed, especially in the dark, swishing mud and trees down to the delta. The river is the ancient soul of Vientiane. The Presidential Palace and the houses of the Lao elite faced onto it. During the May Rocket Festival to glorify Buddha and ask for spring rains, large decorated rockets of bamboo are shot over the river while the men drink, paint their faces, and sing bawdy songs. The river was always our destination, and then we turned home.

Houses: Ours and Others

Our house was so new that the street had no name known to the local residents. This was no handicap, since it was easy to find. From the monument, head toward That Luang, take the first dirt road to the left, and look for the first white house on the left. Letters from home did not get lost because our mailing address was our office in the U.S. government compound in town.

There was nothing distinctive or native about the style of our house—it could have been in Long Beach, California—but it was designed to make efficient use of breeze and space. A small garden spread across the front, from the driveway and latticed cement breezeway for our secondhand car to the low white side wall over which we could see the houses and water towers of our neighbors a rice field away. Sectioned by concrete and metal runners to hold the earth in place, the garden flowers were grouped in tropical varieties, bright red, purple, and pink, surrounded by long, sharp-tipped leaves or spiked ferns. The garden really belonged to Loc, our Vietnamese cook, who took obvious pleasure in keeping it watered and fertile. The only other resident who did more than walk through the place was our Siamese kitten Minou, who spent several hours a day meditating under the broadest leaves and ferns.

All white concrete, the house began with a brief concrete-latticed front porch that was too hot in the day or too buggy in the evening to sit on. The front door opened onto a living room–dining room area with a floor of inlaid, interwoven dark and light wood that caught the sunlight in changing and intricate patterns. The windows suited the climate perfectly. Against outside screens, they were louvered glass that opened and closed like venetian blinds to adapt to both breezes and heavy rains. Our second Siamese kitten Sam fit perfectly between the opened louvers when he first arrived and he slept there during breezes after the rainstorms until he grew too large.

The walls were white plaster with built-in shelves of the same honey-colored wood as in the floor, and all the furniture was rattan with plain cushions. On the floor were two beige Indian wool rugs with birds and animals and flowers stitched in soft colors. Around the room on shelves and two-tiered coffee tables we kept books, thriving plants, and low globe-shaped lamps without shades. These were difficult to read by because they beamed a stark white light in your eyes rather than on the page. In one corner was a vase of tall dried plants, including four long pearl-gray feathery ones the length of horses' tails, that swayed in abundance along the roads outside Vientiane. Leaning across one bookshelf was a Lao *kaen,* a bundle of striped wooden pipes tied together in staggered sizes that when blown screeched and wheezed in high-pitched tones. It was a traditional instrument of the mountain people of northeastern Laos, and even now over twenty years later, it emits a dank, tarry odor suggesting the opium sap that provides these people their major livelihood.

Three other rooms off the dining room completed the house—the tiled kitchen, a small study, and our bedroom and bath. In the study, we kept a Yamaha spinet with an inside lamp to ward off dampness. We also spent weekly sessions there with a French tutor. The kitchen belonged to Loc and Nam, his wife. Both arrived every morning at seven riding double on a black motor scooter and left at eight in the evening. Our bedroom was the only air-conditioned room, with a long bathroom complete with fixtures and a high-sided tub of the same rose and black speckled material as our tub in Saigon. The back window of the bedroom faced the low white wall dividing our yard from a rice field and huts, beyond which ran That Luang road to town.

Some of the other Vientiane houses rented by Westerners were of a different nature. One of our colleagues lived by himself in a house built by a Chinese developer, a high, garishly painted two-story structure of dark wood walls, bewildering room arrangements and closets, and long, wasted hallways. The entire house seemed entirely uncomfortable no matter what room or piece of furniture one tried. Another colleague lived along the river in an old four-room wooden structure covered with flowering vines and open to river breezes, mosquitoes, and anyone walking along the street. A third, also a single man, preferred a comfortable apartment in a three-story building full of flowerpots and caged birds and French-speaking Lao civil servants, foreign journalists, and embassy employees.

The house of a USAID couple on leave that we rented the first two weeks of our stay was a low wooden structure under tall trees, with a screened porch across the entire front and latticed slats underneath. I kept waiting for chipmunks to dart out of the crisscross openings, because twenty years earlier I used to watch for them coming out of the same kind of latticing that fronted my grandparents' cottage in the mountains.

Of the two highest-ranking Americans whose homes I remember, one was a U.S. Army colonel who lived in a French-built villa with a gravel driveway a short bicycle ride from the center of Vientiane. The other was that of the USAID director and his wife, who rented the large split-level villa along the Mekong built by one of the Royal Lao Government elite. It had wide reception rooms and deep porches that opened onto the river.

The most controversial living quarters for Americans was Kilometer Six, an area outside of town cordoned off by armed guards and built especially to house visiting experts who had come to advise the Lao in agricultural and development matters. The rationale for such a place was that these experts could not really disseminate their expertise to full advantage if also asked to make radical adjustments in their living standards. In addition, the argument went, flooding the slow-moving Lao economy with relatively affluent foreigners would raise rental and consumer prices to an unhealthy level. Each time we visited Kilometer Six we discussed the pros and cons of such a setup for Americans. My personal assessment at the time was that the confining army-base atmosphere and siege mentality, with only compatriots as neighbors just a few yards on every side, would nurture a frame of mind as little conducive to work in Laos as I could imagine.

Aliens

The Vietnamese always must have felt they had to tread lightly in Laos, taking care that what they considered their natural superiority in cultural development and resourcefulness not intimidate the Lao into withdrawal and noncooperation. I met only four Vietnamese in Vientiane. Loc and Nam had arrived there a few years before starting work for us, but due to Loc's severe dignity and taciturn manner, I never knew their story—why they came, what family they had, and what their plans were.

Nam was a plump woman in her forties, with black hair wound tightly at the back of her head in the traditional Buddha mound. She was always in an ironed white blouse, loose black pants, and rubber thongs, which she removed as soon as she entered our door. She spoke only a few words of French and bustled around our small house on her serving and cleaning chores, smiling whenever I looked her way and doting on our new kitten.

Because of the language barrier, Nam's natural deference to Loc for all household arrangements, and her shyness, I never had an extended talk with her. I wonder now what she thought of me, who, like her, was trying to make a temporary home in a foreign culture. She seemed to be a simple woman and I guessed that she was out of touch with the political complications among her country, Laos, and mine, and that she simply was following her husband to find better work in a more peaceful place. If so, I hoped she had relatives and friends around her, because she had a naturally tender and sympathetic nature. One time, a stray and obviously sick tabby cat came to the kitchen door and ate the scraps Nam left him on a newspaper. I still cringe at my over-reaction to this. Because I was worried about his infecting our new kitten, I told Nam in an unnecessarily harsh tone that she should stop encouraging him, then I scooped him up while she watched with sad eyes, put him in the car, and dropped him off in a field a mile away near a cluster of huts. Nam probably concluded that this bizarre behavior was due to a stinginess about dispensing food.

A second incident must have confirmed her feeling that I was strange when it came to cats. When we returned from a two-week visit to Thailand and Malaysia, Loc and Nam seemed glad we were back, especially Nam, who was more animated than usual. Then upon seeing our kitten, who had grown larger and darker—as a Siamese of that age naturally does in that length of time—I knelt down and patted her tentatively, insisting that this was not the same cat. Loc looked worried, as if I were accusing him of something, but Nam laughed—the only time I heard her do so—and seemed to understand my temporary disorientation. I laughed too, and decided she was happy with her job.

Loc was a good cook of the simple soups and dishes we asked of him, especially considering the limited food available in the Vientiane market. The only three preparations I remember are his Vietnamese noodle soup with vegetables and chicken at lunchtime—which left a smooth, spicy aftertaste and beads of sweat on our foreheads—a whole fish stuffed with shrimp and crabmeat and decorated with green vegetables, and the Vietnamese spring rolls with hot fish sauce that he prepared for a musicale in our living room.

He was about fifty, a chain-smoker (which he made sure to do outside the house) with a sharp face, close-cropped head, and bad teeth. A full examination at the hospital pronounced him in sound health. Once he told Joe, with a rueful shake of the head, that the Lao had *"trop de baci"* (too many festivals) and indicated that they were hard to take seriously. Loc's brow was the smoothest when he worked on his garden in our front yard. He dug patches in circular patterns and planted large bell-shaped red flowers and clumps of small purple-pink blossoms that grew in exuberance and closed up in the dark. Although my communication with him was limited to food and serving matters, I liked the sound each morning of his motorbike misfiring as it came up our driveway and the sight of the couple ready to begin their team-work for the day. Loc always wore a blue short-sleeved shirt and brown felt hat with a wide brim. Nam, sitting behind with her arms around his chest, wore dark glasses and a large straw hat tied under the chin with a white sash.

Another Vietnamese was our first real hostess in Vientiane, the cook of the USAID couple whose house we rented our first two weeks. Linh was middle-aged, with dark skin, short hair, and a muscular body. She was not an exceptional cook but was an admirable housekeeper. The evening before her day off, she gave me strict and detailed instructions on how to use an oven and broil a steak. I wondered what kind of luxurious servant-filled life she may have been picturing for me back in the States.

One evening, she told us her story while serving dinner. She stood very still, tensely clenching her hands and repeating phrases over and over in broken French. Her husband had been a colonel in the Vietnamese army of 1949, serving the French, and was shot by the Viet Minh guerrillas because he knew too much. They warned her that if she told the authorities about them, she would be shot also. She kept sticking her finger in her ear and pulling an imaginary trigger as she told us this. She fled to Vientiane, sent her two daughters to France, and had a son working in USAID. Even though she had been in Vientiane for seventeen years, she felt ill at ease and confined there. It was Linh who made our transition to householders an easy one by sending us Loc and Nam.

The last Vietnamese I met was a North Vietnamese army captain who served as an adviser to the Pathet Lao before he was taken prisoner by the Royal Lao Government. He provided valu-able information on the connection between the North Viet-namese and the Pathet Lao. Although I had read all the transcripts of his lengthy interviews, I met him only once in our office. He bounced in with a wide smile and vigorous grip, wear-ing battle fatigues of some kind. At that time or soon afterward, he married a Lao and settled in Vientiane.

Neighbors

On our side of the road across the rice field on our left was a USAID family who seemed to be living a wholesome life in Vientiane. Both parents were learning Lao, sent their son and daughter to Lao-French nursery schools, and entered Vientiane with open eyes and minds. Their six-year-old son had a perfect accent in French and was an avid *Tin-Tin* reader. They had purchased a sweet-natured long-haired brown and white dog named Milou, who returned the abundant affection bestowed on him by the whole family. Almost every morning at eight, we could hear one or the other parent buzzing by on their motor scooter with one child on board on the way to school. I relied on this family for company and conversation during the frequent two- and three-day trips Joe took to the fringes of the war zone in eastern and southern Laos. The family had two Lao girls as servants, with whom they practiced their Lao and established a relaxed working relationship.

Meeting them was also my first encounter with a concerted effort by a family to deal with pesticides and pollutants. Their rationale was that bringing our American notions of an insect-free, disinfectant-sprayed household to Laos was impossible to carry out in a tropical climate, dangerous to children, and destructive to the balance of the natural system. The servants were instructed to scrub the house with a lot of soap and water and to keep screens closed and garbage wrapped in the proper bins, but were asked to launch no murderous campaigns against migrating ants, mosquito-eating lizards, strong cooking odors, and occasional roaches on the front patio.

This novel approach to housekeeping in the tropics piqued my interest in the natural workings of the insect world. One afternoon after lunch, I sat on the wooden floor in front of one white living room wall watching a regiment of medium-size black ants marching in sloppy single file from the baseboard diagonally to the ceiling molding above, where they disappeared. I was reluctant to disturb their concentration but could not resist, in a moment of human arrogance, trying to see whether they could be distracted. I sprayed some deodorant across a small break in their trail. When the first ant came upon it, he or she stopped, turned around, and gave a reconnoitering order to the rest of the troops, then led them in a circular route around the offending roadblock. This route became the permanent roadway for the rest of the regiment, who now marched in a more or less straight line with one diversionary hiccup. I never saw such a troop in our house again, on that wall or any other.

The French couple across the way were polite but remote. I remember only two things about them. One was Monsieur's telling me sadly that several of their cats had died from distemper. The second was their indulgence of my bad French when I met them walking in the marketplace in Luang Prabang with their daughter and answered their question about what I thought of the town with a gushy *"Elle est trés gentille!"*

The Indian family directly across from us were most memorable for their militant geese and for the spicy, smoky smell coming from the incense and cooking that filled their rooms and clothes. I was invited into their house only once. I stepped across the road one evening after dinner when I saw the plump mistress of the house in a dark purple-blue sari walking up and down her front walk holding their month-old first son. His eyes were brilliant and his head a perfectly formed oval, which, she explained, was so shiny because she kept it covered with oil to prevent scalp disease.

After we ran out of baby subjects, she invited me into the entrance room, which was dark and heavily scented. All I can remember of the furnishings was a triangular-shaped altar with flowers and statues, painted bright pink. She and her husband politely discouraged any further overtures from us, and for the rest of our stay we waved pleasantly to each other as we passed in our cars.

The International Set

Our social contacts in Vientiane were almost exclusively other foreign residents. The liveliest, least formal occasions were the Sunday-morning badminton brunches at the villa of the USIA director. The white cement badminton court lined in bright red was the vibrant center of the broad lawn, and provided the entire morning's entertainment. At the edges of the lawn, broad-leaved plants and purple, orange, and red flowering hedges grew beside a white picket fence, beyond which tall trees and underbrush were so impenetrable, you imagined you were staring through a jungle. Here, we were all Americans and therefore relaxed in a way we could not on any other occasion in Vientiane.

The badminton games, which began around nine and finished at noon, were strenuous and serious, the test being not one's level of play but rather the level of enthusiasm and effort you were willing to put forth in ninety-degree temperatures and steady sun. I had spent many childhood hours playing family badminton in the backyard, by loose rules, but this was no preparation for the fast play we encountered on these Sunday mornings. It was most enjoyable to watch the men, who wrapped kerchiefs around their heads and sweated off pounds as they threw themselves around the court in a range of positions from clumsy to artistic. The most formidable player was a former professional athlete in his thirties. In one of our photographs, he is slamming a shot while in the squatting position of a dancing Cossack.

I preferred sitting on the metal-frame lawn chairs, drinking fruit juice and talking to the company gathered around the court. Most of the time, these were Americans in their twenties and early thirties, several of them married couples, who worked for USAID and International Voluntary Service in the towns and mountain villages of Laos.

A number of them worked with a, by that time, legendary Midwestern American farmer in his sixties who was devoting his life to the Hmong and training these young volunteers. He sometimes appeared in Vientiane at the home of a physician couple who were older versions of the dedicated couples we met at the badminton brunches. This physician couple had worked in other underdeveloped areas of the world and were treating the Hmong. The wife had befriended a puppy while living in one of the Hmong villages and then discovered the dog had rabies. The equanimity with which she endured the subsequent series of thirteen painful rabies injections was one indication of her dedication. Her husband gave us a Hmong ceremonial sword of black steel with a wooden carved handle and sheath, and a black rifle with a thin barrel and inlaid wood and bone grip. He said at the time, "Remember that people who make weapons like these will defend their independence to the death."

When the young set of Americans working with the mountain people talked together on our Sunday badminton mornings, they asked thoughtful questions about the political purposes of the U.S. and Royal Lao governments and the course of the war, particularly among the tribes whom they were trying to help. I liked sitting next to the Indonesian wife of one of the American IVS members. She held their golden-skinned four-month-old daughter on her lap, and talked about raising children and working for the Peace Corps, while pushing strands of dark hair behind her ears.

Our host on those Sundays was distinguished-looking even in the midst of a badminton shot. He had graying sideburns, a lean build, and a natural flair for telling stories with tasteful irony, aided by gestures with a cigarette holder. He told one of his longest and best dinner table stories on the occasion of his wedding anniversary. He described his courtship of his wife, ending with a Hollywood finish: he had given his competitor until sundown to get out of town.

They had a teenage son living with them and I vaguely remember him as being handsome and driving around Vientiane in a red convertible. His parents described several times a common problem of teenagers of foreign-service families. They lack the natural peer group they would have back home and seek out whatever peers are available, which in this case, the parents added, tended to be long-uprooted and spoiled French teenagers who grew up with a colonial perspective on Laos. They worried that although such a way of life could be enriching, it was usually more a disorientating, even unhealthy, one for an American still developing.

Our hostess was shy, which she covered by speaking bluntly and laughing in loud bursts. She played a dogged game of badminton and always seemed glad that we were all there on her lawn. Five years later we met their daughter, who was living in the town where we spend our summers. Our other long-term connection with this family was that they gave us Minou, the last of their litter of Siamese kittens.

Our second kitten, Sam, was also a connection with friends. He was given to us by a USAID couple who were both experienced in the foreign service—particularly the wife, whose father had been a U.S. ambassador in Latin America. She met us at the airport on our arrival and saved me a great deal of time in learning how to pay servants, where to get my hair cut, and where to find a reliable doctor. She was adept at lively, warm small talk and I always liked following her around at cocktail parties because she filled in potentially awkward spaces with a musical voice and graceful words. She was inveterately cheerful but I often wondered afterward how much she really enjoyed her role as American hostess in Vientiane.

The other American I came to know well worked on our project and was the wife of a CIA officer. She was a petite person in her thirties with short, straight dark hair and bangs. The couple had a young son, on whom she showered her sentiments, quiet sense of humor, and discipline. It was while talking to her one day as she was giving him a bath that I first learned about Phisohex for bathing in the tropics, to prevent infection.

She played a solid, graceful game of tennis but explained

once that she almost never won because she lacked the killer instinct. At the office, she was a fast, accurate typist and a natural organizer of our activities and material. Her most frustrating task was typing transcripts of taped interviews, some of which were garbled in sound or spoken at too fast a rate to be understood. She developed a keen ear for nuances in peoples' speaking styles and was able to untangle sounds that none of the rest of us could make out, even when listening to our own voices.

Once she mentioned that her family was Greek, which explained her intense dark eyes. Her eyes turned down slightly, giving them an expression totally unrelated to the sunniness of her character. She was self-deprecating, usually with a humorous twist. One time at the office, she hung her head in mock despair at her own unoriginality when I informed her that Cristabel, a name she thought she had just that minute made up, was the title of a poem by Coleridge. Another day, a week before she was due to go on home leave, she admitted with some embarrassment, hidden behind a great *show* of embarrassment, that they were returning to the United States by freighter because she was afraid to fly.

Vientiane was an international marketplace in 1967, with diplomats from the Western, Eastern and neutralist blocs, private businessmen, UN observers, International Control Commission members, private voluntary agencies, intelligence agents, academics, and journalists. All were eyeing each other at various levels of competition and cooperation, to determine how to best carry out their missions. All this attention and enterprise was turned on a pleasant, slow-moving people whose government benefited in the direction of more and larger cars for its officials, a beefed-up military establishment, and a rise in the inflation rate.

One of the most popular places for this set of foreigners to meet casually was the tennis club at the Vientiane stadium. The level of play was not intimidating. I was unwilling to take a chance on looking bad and I just practiced on the sidelines. Among the women players, the French were the most ruthless competitors, their seriousness alleviated by a player from South Africa who laughed frequently and trilled her *r*'s like a Scot.

Among the Americans, a frequent winner of tournaments was a U.S. Army wife who always wore white tennis dresses cut to display her deeply tanned, well-rounded shoulders and legs. Sometimes we played mixed doubles with an American embassy official and his wife. I associate her most clearly with the pillows she once showed me in their living room, made of deep purple and red Indian woven cloth that had pieces of reflecting colored glass sewn into it.

One afternoon, among the group of loud, cheerful onlookers at these tennis matches, I met a German woman who was married to the top-ranking Lao tennis player. I walked with her and her Canadian friend one early morning on a dusty road on the outskirts of Vientiane, listening to her talk about how much she missed her brothers and her seaport home with its brisk weather. She said it was difficult to fit in with the traditional customs of her Lao husband and in-laws, particularly her husband's long daily visits with his family without her, and his strange new attitude of hostility to her demands that he spend more time with her. She watched in a desultory manner as her son and daughter ran ahead of us down the road and she worried that they were getting sick too often.

The only official coffee I remember attending was an affair at the Indian embassy given in honor of the wife of Souvanna Phouma, the premier of Laos. As I was sitting in a circle of women balancing my cup and trying to think of something to say, my eyes were caught by a familiar oval face of a woman across the room. I recognized her from a photograph in our album of a Thai graduate student Joe had known in Geneva eighteen years before, whom I had never met. When I rushed over to her to make the connection and express my wonderment at the coincidence, she received me with a nervous and barely polite "Oh yes" and then looked bored.

When we biked over to the Thai embassy the next day to try again—her husband was Thai ambassador to Laos—she was remarkably changed, eager to renew memories of Geneva. She even made some mischievous remarks about one of the Lao dignitaries at the coffee, despite disapproving looks from her husband. We never saw them again after that visit.

My contacts with the French were brief. One was the newly married, very young wife of a cultural attaché in his fifties. She was supposed to be tutoring me in French. Several afternoons a week, I bicycled to their slightly run-down villa and went through a few textbook lessons with her. The exercise seemed to make her restless, as did her whole Vientiane existence. She soon broke off to talk about herself. When she found out I knew how to play bridge, she proposed devoting our sessions to the game with some of her acquaintances, promising I would be learning a great deal of French during play. But I decided at that point to join with Joe and his tutor, who was a woman of a completely different sort.

A widow in her fifties with a bolt-upright posture, graying hair pulled into a rolled topknot, and wire-rim glasses, she conducted her French sessions with military efficiency. She spent most of her time commenting on Joe's oral translations of French and American news articles and editorials, correcting both his grammar and the opinions of the writers. I was shocked when she told me she was going to write to her family to have their German shepherd destroyed because she had decided he missed her too much. When she once turned with annoyance to our new kitten playing in the corner and said, "Il me distrait," I wondered what she had in mind.

Our one other French contact was a couple who lived in a villa near the airport. He was a military attaché, a colonel, with a conservative, old-fashioned manner and stiff dignity. The day we went to lunch at their villa, he was in full uniform and talked of his birthplace in Martinique. I had trouble picturing him among the rough mountains, black volcanic beaches, and brilliant colors that I remembered of that island. They invited us to return sometime to play bridge.

One group of Americans who never appeared at any social functions were the missionaries, some of whom had been in Southeast Asia for most of their adult lives. We had one dinner with two French priests who had served in Laos for ten years and exhibited the same good humor, commitment, and pragmatism as others we met subsequently. One evening, we biked along the river to the city outskirts to visit an American priest Joe had met on a plane seven years earlier. This priest had spent his ten years in Laos building schools and churches in small villages and mountain areas. He looked like the high tree with rough bark that arched over his wooden house, and spoke in an even, almost monotonous voice with a heavy Texas accent. He told us some horror stories about Pathet Lao treatment of priests, increasing the intensity by addressing us directly by name every few sentences, and smiling. He repeated several times that he thought that our refugee project (which was our cover for studying the Pathet Lao) was going to be important.

One missionary group who appeared everywhere we traveled were the Mormons. They were all young and serious, always in white shirts or blouses, traveling in twos and threes, their expressions abstracted and undisturbed by their environment.

The Lao

One afternoon I was sitting with wet hair facing the mirror in a beauty salon run by a French-speaking Vietnamese woman who was considered the best stylist in town. She had asked me to wait between the wash and set stages while she tended to another customer two chairs away. Looking for something to read, I picked up a thick book—a novel in English—that was leaning against the mirror in front of the empty chair next to me. I don't remember the contents, except that it was an historical romance.

After a few minutes, I felt a stare from two chairs down coming at me through the mirror, and looked up, to meet the cold eyes of a Lao woman in her early thirties. She was surrounded by the patroness and two helpers, who were murmuring into her ear and combing her black hair into a formal upsweep. Still maintaining our eye contact through the mirror, without our exchanging a word or gesture, I realized after some seconds that the book I had picked up was hers. I laughed at what seemed an innocent mistake, said "Excuse me," and set it back in its place against the mirror.

The owner's face was immobile during this short event. She turned her eyes back to her own reflection and the hovering stylists. After she was ushered out the door, the patroness returned to my chair and whispered with some impatience, "That was Her Royal Highness." And that was my only brush with Lao royalty, admittedly indirect since we communicated through a mirror. That was also the nearest I came to experiencing hostile behavior from a Lao. Perhaps it was proper for her to assert her status in front of the Vietnamese patroness and Lao employees, by behaving imperiously toward foreigners, especially those ignorant of the respect due Lao royalty. At the time, my feeling was that I was age eight, dressing up with my cousins in our mothers' old gowns and playing "princess" on our front porch.

The number-one and number-two ranking tennis players of Laos appeared at the tennis tournaments in the Vientiane stadium from time to time. Both were in their late twenties but differed markedly in personality. Number one had a silent, stern manner on and off the court, although he did not really need it for the social matches I saw him play, since there was no one playing at his level. Maybe his hunched shoulders and frowns were due to frustration at the thought that he was losing his skills. His German wife seldom appeared at the tennis club, although one morning around 6:30, she and I hit a few desultory rallies.

The number-two player, who was also the doubles partner of number one, was serene and smiling and, unlike his partner, seemed to enjoy the bantering and social contacts with foreigners that the Vientiane stadium provided. He was a geographer who had studied in France and married a French physician. He had a reflective style in conversation and liked to probe for one's personal philosophy. During the French era in Laos, when he was in his teens, he was a member of the Lao nationalists, the Lao Issara, and had lived in Thailand with Souphanouvong, Lao Issara Minister of Defense at that time.

Years later, Joe was participating in a panel organized by Amnesty International in Paris, speaking about human rights in Laos. During the question period, a woman asked about Lao government policy toward the reeducation camp detainees and identified herself as the wife of a Lao being held in such a camp. Joe was dumbfounded when he realized that she was the wife of the former tennis player and geographer. They went out for coffee afterward and talked about her husband and sons.

The only large Lao official event that I recall was a black-tie Rotary Club affair, put on with fanfare at the Hotel Lan Xang along the river. The Lao dignitaries included Prime Minister Souvanna Phouma and his wife—both of whom left before our arrival—and the Lao ambassador to the U.S.S.R., who wore a heavy black silk mandarin jacket embroidered with whirls of gold and red flowers and who strode through the crowd with a fixed and brilliant smile. The only glimpse I had of Souvanna Phouma was during a parade down Lan Xang Avenue, when he marched with his government officials, all in white coats and long, traditional skirts.

My brush with the finance minister of the Royal Lao Government was as a guest at one of his family mansions on the river—and as a spectator at a badminton doubles match he set up with Joe and the USAID director. The minister brought as his partner a Lao national champion, whose excessive youth and skill, matched by the minister's excessively refined and arrogant style, made their victory a foregone conclusion.

Most Lao women I saw only from a distance. In the street, I admired their small-boned figures, which they maintained much past middle age, aided by the grace of their slim silk skirts, reaching to the ankles. The most important part of the skirt was the bottom border, where the designers let free their imaginations by creating swirling flower designs or a series of bands of gold and silver threads. Class distinctions in dress resided in the choice of jewelry, the quality of the dress material, and whether the wearer was shod in simple thongs or in leather dress shoes of European design.

My other place of contact with Lao society were the large parties put on by U.S. Embassy personnel. The Lao officials' wives often did not appear at all, sending polite messages through their husbands that they were ill. When they did come to these affairs, sitting together in one large stiff group, I decided after trying a few times to initiate a conversation that I would burden them less if I smiled and moved on.

There was only one Lao woman with whom I had extended contact, since she worked on our project. She was from a distinguished family. Her uncle had been a leader of the Lao Issara and prime minister of the Lao government in exile during that period. She was newly married and gave birth to her first child during the time we were there. We spoke in French, as she had been a student at the Sorbonne, where she met her husband, a young Lao official. My French was not severely taxed because my conversations with her in the office always remained pleasant, relaxed, and superficial.

I don't remember how many direct personal questions I may have asked her, like what she thought about the government in Laos or the U.S. presence there, or what she hoped for her new child, or how she felt about her experience in France. In any case, she has left only a fragile mark on my memory—a pretty, modestly dressed young woman, her long hair tied back simply, her head always down over her job of translating her uncle's memoirs.

I last visited her after her son was born. I sat next to her in the dark parlor of her house, with her mother and aunt standing nearby, smiling and nodding. I congratulated them all on the perfection and robust health of the sleeping new baby. His mother held him in her lap, bending over him and never breaking the silence.

Loeillet, Mozart, Bach

One evening, a month after our arrival in Vientiane, I participated in my first Soirée Musicale at the home of a U.S. Embassy couple (who a few months earlier conducted what must have been the first bar mitzvah in Vientiane). My partners were two flutists who were radically different from each other. One was an English teacher who had lived in Vientiane for over five years. He was a quiet man, tall and stooping, with large hands and forearms, light receding hair, and light eyes. He loved cats and birds and his musical tone was singularly lilting. He never directly criticized any of my piano renditions, even when, at that first performance, I started a Vivaldi concerto in double time. He stopped, smiled, and asked to start over.

In conversation, he revealed nothing about his past or his judgments on present topics. If the conversation became too dangerous, he turned his head aside and stepped back a few paces. He left those who knew him slightly with the feeling that he was inordinately sensitive and protecting himself from pain.

His fellow flutist was also a teacher, a Frenchman of great vigor and abruptness who drove the most comical car in Vientiane—an old dishwater-color Renault Deux Chevaux that bounced and rattled down Vientiane's dusty roads with an air of impeturbability. He had lived in Laos most of his life. His wife was a poised Vietnamese and his son a combination of both parents, with his mother's eyes and his father's dark square-top crew cut, dark brows, and outgoing manner.

By different means, this flutist also fended off personal questions, turning the conversation to barbed, impatient remarks about the conduct of foreigners among the Lao or witty comments on the French connotation of his name, which literally was the name of an insect. He never seemed very pleased with our practice sessions and periodically referred to a piano accompanist he had had who always followed him perfectly. His best performance, which I accompanied, was a Mozart concerto in which his vigorous technique, fast pace, and clarity of tone showed to best advantage.

The three of us performed three times over eight months— a Vivaldi concerto at the bar mitzvah household in February, and Loeillet, Mozart, and Bach at two Soirées Musicales at our house in June. I practiced every day on the spinet we had purchased from a U.S. Embassy family and made sure the tone was right for the flutists by commissioning a blind piano tuner from Bangkok who made periodic trips to Vientiane. He was surprisingly young and played American songs of the forties as he checked the intervals and action. I made a tape of my orchestral accompaniment to the Mozart—and have been surprised in subsequent years at hearing the level of proficiency I had reached with steady practice, which I have not matched since.

We decided to hold the event twice in our living room to accommodate all the people the three of us wanted to invite— about fifteen to twenty people each evening. We moved the piano beside the front door and I tacked to the back of it, facing the audience, our honeycomb-patterned orange and purple batik cloth bought seven years before in Indonesia. I wrote home at the time that the first evening seemed more exciting, although our performance was better on the second. I recall cringing at mistakes while performing and then exchanging a look of dissatisfaction from the Frenchman and a smile of relief from the American at the end of each piece. The tape of the performance records some nice moments and some clear weaknesses.

I gave a lot of thought to what I would wear for each occasion. I chose two materials we had bought in Singapore two months earlier—a sheer white Indian cotton with a blue, green, and rose border and a purple, green, and black cotton batik. A local seamstress cut and sewed both dresses just as I requested, with a scoop neck and bare arms. I can see from the photographs that both dresses had problems in conforming to waist and shoulders—but then so did most of the flowered and patterned dresses worn by the other women at the party. For Western women in Vientiane, there was almost always a large disparity between an exquisite local material as it first looked on the bolt and the final look once we were wearing it.

Our audience sat along the walls on our various pieces of rattan furniture and dining room chairs and took the canapés and drinks Loc passed around on trays during the break. There were friends and colleagues from work, embassy and USAID officials, the USIA director, our French tutor, a visiting CBS journalist, neighbors, a Canadian official with the United Nations, a German physician, and an American scholar studying Lao and Cambodian history in the local archives. In our photographs, the faces of the audience are intent and purposeful.

The Ancient Royal Capital

The Mekong carved out another narrow river valley to the north of Vientiane that became Luang Prabang, the ancient royal capital of Laos. It maintained its status as the seat of royalty through five centuries of coalescence and fragmentation of the Lao kingdoms. Prince Fa Ngoun, who unified the territories of what is present-day Laos, established his court at Luang Prabang (Town of the Golden Buddha) in the fourteenth century. The city was named for the two-and-one-half-foot-high golden statue of the standing Buddha, called the Prabang, that Fa Ngoun had enshrined there after his conversion to Buddhism. Two hundred years later, Vientiane was designated the royal capital for a brief period, until the wrangling Lao states split into three separate kingdoms, one of them being Luang Prabang.

In 1886, the Siamese granted France the right to send a vice-consul to Luang Prabang in order to protect her from Vietnamese claims—and the French thereby established colonial control of Laos in the person of Auguste Pavie. When a White Thai chieftain attacked Luang Prabang the next year and burned it to rubble, Pavie saved the life of the old Lao king and persuaded him to accept France as its new protector in place of Siam. Under the French, Luang Prabang was retained as the royal seat of Laos, while Vientiane became the administrative capital, the link between the two cities not completely forged until 1943 when the French completed the Royal Road connecting them.

Although the real power resided elsewhere than with the royal families, rivalries among them for control of the royal seat in Luang Prabang continued through the French colonial period, the Japanese invasion in the early 1940s, and the rise of Lao nationalism. In 1941, King Sisavang Vong signed a treaty with the French that extended his authority to all of northern Laos, under a French protectorate. He was deposed four years later by the Lao nationalists, then restored by them to his throne in Luang Prabang at the end of World War II.

After his death in 1959, his successor, King Savang Vatthana, worked with the bewildering changes of government in Laos that took shape with the introduction of American influence. He made appointments to government positions at the dictates of his Lao, American, French, British, and Australian advisers. By 1967, the growing civil war between the Communists and the Royal Lao Government inside Laos and the looming Vietnam War across the border rendered the royal house of Luang Prabang increasingly fragile and irrelevant.

The king's palace in Luang Prabang is modest in size and design, particularly when first viewed from the mountaintop wat that overlooks the town a few hundred feet above the river. Our host, an American working for the U.S. Information Agency, pointed down through silver branches sprouting white blossoms and the dark green treetops of palm, pine, and eucalyptus to a low rectangular building along the Mekong. The central entrance was a single front door under an arching black roof crowned by a golden swirl shaped like a pagoda. The grass and trees surrounding the one-story wings that spread on either side of the doorway were well clipped and watered and the grounds were minimally enclosed on the road side by a low stone wall and a gate of bright red iron gratings, with no guard in sight.

The rest of the town that spread below us along the river looked asleep through the haze of that hot afternoon. The river was low, with a few long sculls resting halfway up the banks, and occasional bicycle and animal traffic moved slowly on the roads, with no sounds reaching our ears.

Our host, the chief American presence in Luang Prabang, was operating a small kingdom of his own. He was about thirty, tall and husky, with a large face and square jaw. His unguarded facial expressions and slow manner of speaking won him immediate friends among the Lao. He spoke fluent Lao, which he first learned as a Peace Corps volunteer in northern Thailand. As he introduced us to the two servants in his villa in the hills above the town, to Italian priests running a boys school nearby, to the wats and sights of Luang Prabang, to a village outside the town, to a Vietnamese pagoda, he was always greeted with smiles and people constantly took him by the hand and arm. He had a full library on Lao culture and history. He spoke with humor and some irony about his own work in Luang Prabang, explaining that he would probably stay there indefinitely. We heard a year later that he had been killed in a plane crash while accompanying Lao students to Ban Hoei Sai on a small U.S. military plane in which he had arranged to take them home.

The wat we visited was an especially ornate and sparkling example of the Lao dedication to Buddha. Red, gold, green, and white dominated. Young novitiate bonzes wrapped in light and dark gold cotton robes, their heads shaved, sat or walked among white stone stupas spaced generously around the grounds among thick trees and bushes sprouting red blossoms. Some of the stupas were elaborately gilded and carved with delicate spires of gold emerging out of flame-shaped bases.

The major temple was a wooden structure with swooping roofs that finished in gold serpent heads at the eaves and peaks. Along the sides and across the doorways was a fantasy of gilded floral patterns, filigreed archways, stupa shapes, mythical figures, people working at prosaic tasks, and plants and animals—all in exuberant celebration. In the sun, the effect was brilliant, the light reflecting off the tiny pieces of colored glass and gilt that anonymous craftsmen had embedded and continually renewed in the wood and cement of the temple walls.

This galaxy of color and form demanded closer scrutiny. I spent ten minutes studying one mural, a tree trunk and branches set into a deep red wall and branching symmetrically to the roof. This tree was hung with tear-shaped leaves and flowers and guarded on either side by peacocks, turned in silhouette, although their tails were fully spread and facing front. The tree seemed to be actually moving continually upward because of the subtly changing light and color of the pieces of glass along its trunk, from black-green at the roots to the final sky-blue branches on top. At the center of the trunk was a branch on either side that seemed to be in flame at the tip, under which each guardian peacock was stationed. Like the entire wat, the scale was human-size and the vision joyful.

We visited a Vietnamese pagoda that was plain and dingy by comparison, with one large sitting Buddha under an umbrella its only decorative aspect. We leaned over the parapet with our host and watched the bonzes wind down to the river to wash, their robes making flower spots among the rocks. Our final religious visit was to a school for boys, run by two priests who seemed an invincible team. They were both young, handsome, and smiling, one French and one Italian, one in black robe and the other in white with a black sash. They showed us their new two-story building and rows of boys in clean uniforms, explaining in soft, energetic French why they were needed in such a place.

Our last day in Luang Prabang, our host drove us in his jeep along a red road that sprayed us with a fine dust to a village set in hills of jungle palm and banyan trees. The villagers clustered out to meet us, eager to look at the photographs that our host had taken of them and was distributing. One girl of seven with a harelip was awestruck when she saw her picture. The houses were lined up in a compound, clean and dry on stilts. Daytime activities, including weaving and cooking, took place underneath. The people we saw were in the same postures and doing the same tasks as those pictured in glass and gold on the walls of the wat we had visited the day before.

One villager in a dark long-sleeved shirt and green plaid skirt posed for our picture. He faced full front with arms at his side, standing beside the ladder leading to his front doorway. The fence circumscribing a corral around the base of the house suggests that he owned some animals and that this was private property. His military stance cut a sharp shadow across the red dirt ground.

On the Milk Run

One weekend we flew to Savannakhet, a river town several hours south of Vientiane along the Lao-Thai border. This was my first flight in a cargo plane, a trip somewhat like sitting inside the rib cage of a low-flying bird. Under the spine and side braces of the single unpressurized cabin, the passengers sat facing each other with their backs braced against the vibrating side walls, looking across piles of freight strapped to the floor. The most disconcerting event in flight was the moment when one of the freight crew slid open a door to toss out some coffee cups.

We stayed in a hotel with a Lao name that means "very comfortable." It had a two-story high, open doorway and a spacious, damp reception room with a single lamp and reception desk that was seldom occupied. I do not remember seeing other guests there that weekend, and when in our room, I spent most of my time mopping up the flooded bathroom floor with a towel. The place had the relaxing atmosphere of gentle decay.

Sunday afternoon, we lunched and swam with the local USIA officer and a group of young American IVS volunteers. The lunch place seemed deserted, with no signs of Lao anywhere. It was a former French military base with a few barracks and a murky green swimming pool with floating leaves on the surface and a two-tiered diving platform that was freshly painted. The volunteers lounged on the diving boards and talked about their work in the southern Laos region. The absolute quiet around us and the look of disuse about the place gave the impression that they must have been talking about events in the distant past. It was difficult to imagine that there was presently anything for them to do in Savannakhet.

The one reminder of French days was the swashbuckling French commandant with whom we talked outside his cement barracks, which was covered with bougainvillea. He was dark and thin, dressed in a loose blue shirt and brief white shorts, and talked with caged energy. He had spent his life serving in the French army both in Indochina and Algeria, where he was a ardent member of the OAS. Imprisoned in 1960 for his belligerent defense of "une Algérie française," he was given the choice of remaining in prison or serving as commandant of this defunct military base in Savannakhet. He pointed to a jagged dark brown scar along his inner thigh and explained that Viet Minh shrapnel had given him that, which welded him to Southeast Asia. He considered his present post a justification for the saga of his life as a French soldier.

Bouns and Parades

One of the Lao employees of an international organization—who must have had a French education, judging by her
short skirts, high heels, flirtatious manner, and introduction to
strangers as Mademoiselle—invited us to a *baci* in honor of her
twenty-first birthday. (A *baci,* a ceremony of prayers and good
wishes that predates the arrival of Buddhism in Laos, is a type of
Lao *boun* or festival, which our Vietnamese cook claimed occurred too often among the Lao.) In a low room, about twenty of
us sat on the floor on straw mats around a center floral piece in a
silver bowl. The bowl was filled with long stalks of yellow flowers, which were also strung in trails along the floor and were
surrounded by bottles of rice wine, small cakes, and hard-boiled
eggs. An old man with roughly cut gray hair and a plaid silk sash
across his chest sat across from the birthday celebrant, who was
dressed in a traditional red and gold silk skirt. The old man
chanted prayers in a soft monotone, nodding his head periodically
toward the guest of honor.

We all joined hands during this ceremony and were told
later that the prayers were also being directed toward the Westerners among us, asking that no evil befall us during our visit to
Laos. Afterward, a woman with few teeth and the same face and
cropped hair as the chanter pulled my arms over to her lap and
tied a series of strings around my wrists, mumbling and smiling as
she did so. A translator explained that she was praying that I
would have many sons and daughters.

The air was quiet and amber with the late-afternoon sun
and we talked together in a slow and generous mood.

The most raucous *boun* is the Rocket Festival held during
the period of the full moon in the sixth month of the lunar
calendar. It is to ask Buddha—and before him, the older gods—

for rains to fertilize the spring planting. We walked along the river beside parades of men with rouge and lipstick or faces painted dark green and white, wearing large brimmed hats covered with pink tissue-paper flowers and long Lao skirts. Most had been drinking for hours and listed down the wide dirt road while doing grotesque imitations of the liquid movement of traditional Lao dance.

Other groups of men were somber, particularly the Hmong, who wore long black shirts and pants, scarlet sashes, and thick silver necklaces. One group wore white flour sacks stretched over a barrel frame over their heads and bodies, with eye and nose holes cut out and faint blue labels across the bottom that read, DONATED BY THE UNITED STATES OF AMERICA. Loud music accompanied the reeling motions of the parade, provided by marchers carrying drums under their arms and pipers producing two high-pitched notes that sounded like a large bird in trouble.

We stopped beside a group of novitiate bonzes in saffron robes who were hunkering out of the sun under black umbrellas. The major event was just beginning, the launching of homemade rockets across the river toward Thailand, with the one flying the highest or farthest winning the greatest honor. The one rocket I got close to was made of light wood and orange, red, and green braided streamers of silk and paper. It was launched from the top of a car, and after much advice to its creator from bystanders, it took off with a small explosion behind. My eye could not follow its path because of the trees, brilliant light reflecting off the river, and other rockets being fired. The crowd cheered and the owner looked happy.

As it grew dark, the river took on a deep glow from the occasional flares still being launched over its face and the small fires of people clustered in family groups cooking barbecued chicken along its banks.

The Vientiane Army Day parade brought out the whole society, marching or watching along Lan Xang Avenue, ending at the elephantine monument honoring the war dead, which had been freshly painted for the occasion in Wedgwood blue and white. First came the Royal Lao Government officials in dark skirts, white jackets, and black shoes, surrounding Prime Minister Souvanna Phouma at the center. They walked to a large reviewing stand where the king had already been seated and were joined by military officials and foreign dignitaries, including the strange combination of Soviet, Chinese, North Vietnamese, and American diplomats.

Then followed in parade, Lao boy scouts, schoolchildren, and other groups that walked in no particular order and were difficult to distinguish one from the other. Finally came the army in various types of uniforms. I do not recall seeing any weapons either in their hands or rolling along the road, nor do I remember any marching music. Although people were packed together on the roadside, hunkering along the tops of walls and under red and white striped awnings, there was little cheering or show of enthusiasm for any of the marching groups. Instead, there was a generalized murmuring and thoughtful expressions on peoples' faces.

Pathet Lao Study

Except for the extra nap time to rest from the heat, we kept a regular American workday in Vientiane. We bicycled to the office at 8:30, returning home for lunch, then working until 5 P.M. The office was a set of rooms inside one of the air-conditioned concrete buildings that made up the USAID compound. The compound was something like the set of "Gunsmoke." Low yellow buildings faced each other on either side of one sunny, dusty street. Doorways stood in the deep shadow of overhanging roofs and fence posts marked the spots where cars were to be pulled up, headfirst. Every kind of service was on that one street—the post office, restaurant, movie house, supply building, commissary, and stable of cars and drivers.

The Americans established an active and purposeful work atmosphere and the Lao and Thai employed by them worked cheerfully at the unaccustomed pace, particularly the drivers, who smiled pleasantly through long waits in the heat and sudden emergency runs.

The purpose of our project was to study the Lao Communist movement—the Pathet Lao or PL—through interviews of prisoners and defectors being held by the Royal Lao Government in Vientiane and several other provinces. At that time, the Pathet Lao were trying to gain control of the northeast provinces and the provinces in the southern panhandle through which the Ho Chi Minh Trail passed. In 1967, the nature of their attempt was shifting from political to military as it became increasingly clear that their 1962 coalition with the Royal Lao Government was falling apart. In 1968, a few months after we left Vientiane, the communist forces succeeded in gaining the northeast and spread south. The Pathet Lao army won a major victory at Nam Bac, and North Vietnamese troops overran an American air-directional station sitting on a nine-thousand-foot cliff near the town of Sam Neua.

An important objective of the Americans was to prevent North Vietnamese troops from infiltrating to South Vietnam through eastern Laos. In order to do this, the United States was arming the Royal Lao Government as a bulwark against Vietnamese incursions into Laos along the Ho Chi Minh Trail, while bombing the Trail area relentlessly. Data from our study demonstrated the extent to which the Vietnamese Communists had infiltrated the Pathet Lao. The entire Lao Communist movement was historically, militarily, and politically dependent on North Vietnam, who was "Big Brother," as close to Laos as lips to teeth, as Communist radio broadcasts put it.

Gathering material from these radio broadcasts was one of my major tasks as project administrator and researcher. I spent a few hours a day clipping information relevant to the Pathet Lao from the Foreign Broadcast Information Service, which meant steeping myself in the cement prose of Communist propaganda such as:

> The national front and mass organizations are the important irreplaceable factor in the proletarian dictatorship. That is why our Party and State have the policy to strengthen and broaden the front and to consolidate and improve the organization of the revolutionary mass organizations, to conform to the requirements of the political tasks of the new period.

Lao Communist documents—leaflets, schoolbooks, stories, manifestos, histories—were piled around the desks and tables of our office, waiting to be translated from Lao to English, sometimes with a French version in between. The major data, the interviews with PL prisoners and defectors, had to be processed and coded, after being transcribed from a tape. I particularly liked piecing together biographies and party structure charts of PL leaders, who had fairy-tale names such as Khamouane Boupha and Singkapo Chounlamany, and large, tantalizing gaps in their biographies—first item: born in Savannakhet of Vietnamese father, a peddler, and Lao mother; next item: gunrunner for Lao Issara behind French lines. In my mind, they remain partially sketched out figures for a novel.

Our staff included several transcribers, one secretary, and a few translators. One of the latter was a tall, assertive Vietnamese woman married to an American. She came in a few days a week and interspersed her garrulous personal stories with the production of English versions of Vietnamese. A Lao-speaking Thai from Udorn was the translator for most of the interviews and traveled with the project directors to prisons and detention centers. He must have found this work distressing, or had private troubles, because he always appeared at the office with an anxious frown and drooping head, and seldom spoke.

Since we were dealing with material that had an ambiguous classification status, we office staff worried from time to time about what we could leave on top of our desks, how much we could talk about the data outside the office, and what we should lock up. The codirector would get particularly concerned about this, especially when official visitors were passing through. But he also maintained a sense of humor on the issue. One day after lunch, and after a trying morning of long, elaborate discussions with him about keeping our data both well duplicated and well hidden, I found the following memo from him on my desk, stamped with a U.S. government seal:

> To Project Administrator, Pathet Lao Study: During inspection this morning we found on your desk the attached blank sheet of paper, otherwise unidentified. Be advised that this will be duly recorded on your official record.

Since I was office-based, I did not travel to the province towns and mountain areas as the project directors did. One area I regretted missing was the Hmong country in the central mountains of Laos. Supporting these people had become the special project of the CIA, who considered the Hmong, with their fierce independent spirit, the perfect group to use as a battering ram against Pathet Lao and North Vietnamese troops in eastern Laos. We have twenty-five slides taken during Joe's trip to one Hmong area, which was being administered by a powerfully built CIA operative with a bald head, known among American colleagues as Mr. Clean.

To judge by the slides, he was obviously devoted to his job and the Hmong he was arming and supporting. In one photo, he is standing in casual cotton shirt and shorts, bending toward a group of young Hmong men, the tallest of whom comes only to his shoulder. In another, he is smiling across a swimming pool of freshly built concrete while one naked little boy is poised on a log across the width, about to jump in. In a third, he is talking to a group of children, patting one's shoulder and head, and in a fourth, turning back toward the camera as he walks down a hill on a red dirt path that winds past low fences, dark huts with sweeping thatched roofs, and green scrub and fields in the distance.

The Hmong children are smiling in the photographs, with high color in their cheeks and sculpted features, wearing black skirted garments sashed with chartreuse and pink and heavy silver necklaces. A few have surprisingly light-colored hair and some are wearing sweaters and pants. There are a few dark shots inside the school showing silhouettes of children's heads and white sunlight shining through bamboo-slatted walls. There is one of a prison-camp barracks in the distance against a steep slate-colored hill, and one of two small white instruction planes sitting like Popsicle sticks in a small airfield surrounded by mountain peaks. Three Hmong soldiers pose self-consciously in another shot, two of them wearing army fatigue jackets, and the third, a white shirt and jeans, his red beret the only sign of a uniform.

There is one close-up of opium poppies, the bulbous white flowers standing up in a field of green ferns and protected by a high fence of woven bamboo shafts cut to sharp points at the top.

The landscape shots show a part of Laos I never saw—a river with water buffalo drinking in the foreground and mountains rising immediately on the opposite bank, green scrub and pine alternating with dusty bare ground.

There is one photograph that I always look at the longest. In the middle of a dirt yard lies a sleeping orange dog. It must be high noon, since his sprawled body casts almost no shadow. Farther back are two huts, their sloped thatch roofs almost touching, and still farther back, a dusty and green hill that becomes a jagged blue mountain against a blue and white sky. In the bottom-right foreground stands a Hmong soldier in neatly pressed U.S. Army issue and black boots, his face shaded by the visor of his cap. He faces full front with shoulders squared, arms stiffly at his sides, feet planted slightly apart. He looks hot and uncomfortable.

Canines, Equines, Bovines

The primitive character of Laos that came closest to home was the pack of eight starving, half-wild dogs that roamed the road in front of our house and terrorized small children and pets. They were led by one gray-yellow bitch about the size and shape of a weimaraner; she was probably the mother of most of them, to judge by their similar body types. When she wasn't mating with one of her pack, she was at their center or at the end as they slunk behind the houses at dusk and at night looking for garbage and game.

One evening, the dogs flattened themselves under the gate of our friends down the road and surrounded Milou, their brown and white dog. By the time our friends got out into the yard with rakes, Milou was so torn and bleeding that he could only stare at them with bright eyes for a few minutes and then he died. After that, his owners and I hated those dogs, and the father of the house remarked once that he tried to hit them with his car when they were loping along the roadside.

There seemed to be no Lao official to whom to appeal for handling these beasts—or at least no way of getting an active response from the Vientiane government. The dogs disappeared after two months, either because they moved on to another territory or because, as rumored, some U.S. authorities rounded them up. If the latter was the case, the most the Americans could have done was deposit the pack in some other area, since it was an anathema in the Lao Buddhist culture to destroy animals.

One pet the dogs left alone was a shaggy gray pony with a rope halter who grazed at the edge of the paddy where our road turned toward town. I never knew who his owner was but he had a Lao caretaker in black sarong and bare feet who sat under a straw roof on the other side of the road. One morning, I walked close to the pony and noticed that his leg was bleeding from leeches. When I put my hand on his shoulder, he tossed his head at me in irritation. I walked over to the caretaker to tell him about the leeches, using hand motions, but, of course, he was fully aware of them and saw no reason for action. He smiled, turned his palms to the sky, and said something in Lao that I interpreted as meaning, Don't be silly; there have always been leeches there and the pony is used to them.

The most benign wanderers of our neighborhood were the water buffalo that strolled in groups of two and three past our house and even through our open drive gates. They ignored us when we walked or bicycled near them, although someone passed on to us the traditional warning that buffaloes do not like the smell of Westerners. We honked politely when they were blocking our car's path, and they raised their heavy heads to gaze at us through the windshield with deep liquid eyes, outlined dark and still by the white light of noon or the orange background of sunset.

They were the most precious possessions of the Lao farmers, and pulled the plows and the carts to market. They were local ancient deities, magnificently horned. They had the simple look of rocks, particularly when a boy of four or five sat on their backs as they grazed or a small bird landed on their necks to root insects out of their rough hair.

Minou

We had our first cat in Vientiane. She came to us as a gift from the hosts of our badminton Sunday brunches, who casually asked if we wanted her as she strolled under our chairs and sniffed our bare feet. She was a four-month-old Siamese, plump and round-faced, still mostly pearl white with light blue eyes, her striking deep brown points and mask just beginning. Even at that age, she had a dignified sensitivity and watchful manner that appealed to me. She seemed to suit the soft voices, bright colors and deep shadows, and slow grace of the country and people where she was born.

We have one close-up photograph of her lying in the middle of the Indian wool rug we bought in Vientiane and used in our living room. The rug has a light background the same color as her fur and is embossed with flowers of colored yarn arranged in circular patterns like spokes of a wheel. Minou is lying on her side across the center of one flower wheel, her head slightly raised and looking straight at the camera, her front paws stretched to the left in the eloquent and mysterious gesture of a Hindu carving.

We also have a photograph of her taken a year later in the same pose, although this time the rug is a swirling leaf pattern and she is obviously pregnant.

Her parentage is rooted in Vientiane since her maternal granddam was owned by the American flutist whom I accompanied and her parents were owned by our badminton hosts. Fortunately, she resembled her dam, who was shy, more than her sire, who was huge and had such a nasty temper that when he planted himself in the middle of our hosts' front stairway, we were advised to go around to the back. One time when he flipped on his back and seemed to be inviting play, Joe reached over his head to give him a stomach rub and received three deep claw marks along the wrist and arm that had to be bandaged for days afterward. The only indications we ever had that Minou as a mature cat shared her father's character were her swift manner in killing small rodents, lizards, and birds, and her impulse to run at a small cowardly dog who sometimes wandered onto our front lawn.

She fit into our household as soon as she arrived, making an immediate friendship with Nam, who enticed her into the kitchen for scraps with a soft, high "minou, minou" that sounded to me like the perfect name for a cat. I was not dissuaded from that choice of name by our French tutor, an uncompromising linguist, who informed me that we should change it to "Minette" or "Minousche" since "Minou" was commonly the masculine form.

Minou was invariably happy to see us at the end of our workday and, as is characteristic of Siamese, sought our company constantly and usually discreetly, except for the times she placed herself in the center of something we were trying to read. Her favorite spots were the windowsills of two large windows that formed the front corner of our living room. Inches from the late-afternoon rainstorms, she sat dry and cool, staring across the front lawn at the family of geese rushing back and forth across the way, or out the side past the water buffalo and rice paddy to the traffic on That Luang Road.

At first she went in and out of the house at will, not wandering any farther than a little past the driveway gate. But at nine months, she went into heat and I was advised that if I wanted to wait to breed her, I should keep her in. This was not easy, since her weird cries were continuous through the day and night. The best distraction was the neighboring male cats who came to pay court outside her window. Two were constant—one all black, the other all white, part of the French household down the road.

They stayed outside the window most of the night yowling and dancing and spraying the hedges. Minou sat quietly on her windowsill through most of this show. I remember waking up several times and seeing her composed silhouette against the bright night sky. The second time she went into heat, I drove her around Vientiane in our small car several times and, as I had hoped, the car motion and dusty roads full of people and animals were a temporary distraction.

We decided to find her a mate who would eventually be able to synchronize with one of her heats. From American friends, we obtained Sam, a white two-month old Siamese who promised to be a seal point but who at the time had only a black nose. His parents belonged to the USAID couple who first greeted us at the airport on our arrival in Vientiane. His sire was a large gentle Bluepoint and his maternal granddam the same as Minou's.

He quickly made himself at home and until he grew too large, he chose as his favorite sleeping spot the bottom slat of any window. Whenever anyone walked into the room, he picked up his head for a moment and squinted, a small scrunched-up face beneath huge ears. He was a devilish type, alternating bursts of energy with sudden naps. Minou responded to him like a patient older sister and seemed glad to have his antics to liven up her day.

One afternoon I spent an hour sketching them sleeping together on our green striped bedspread. Sam was on his back with his head against her stomach and one front paw thrown up against her side. What fascinated me was the task of getting right the proportional differences in their sizes—an infant head against a mature one, full-size paws next to growing ones. It is apparent that I had a particular problem with Minou's nearer ear, which tilted out toward the viewer and had to be foreshortened. That drawing now hangs on our stairway and keeps alive Minou and Sam and my hour of concentration.

Miscarriage

Three weeks before we left Vientiane, I had an early miscarriage. When signs first began, we consulted with a respected German doctor in town who sent me to bed with injections and kindly counsel to rest and the assurance that this was the best modern medicine could do. He was cheerful and graying and unhurried, and his visits to the house were comforting, although his diagnosis was that this pregnancy was not meant to be. I requested several books from the British Council Library, including some Dickens, and was kept constant company by the cats and Nam's frequent entrances with meals, broom and mop, and solicitous looks.

I finally had to fly to Bangkok for a D & C with a Thai doctor who was a Johns Hopkins graduate and had a large suite of examining rooms on the ground floor of his villa outside the city. We took a taxi directly there and were greeted hospitably by his wife and servants, although they had not received our telegram that we were coming. The doctor was short and round. I remember the vague outlines of a silly story he was telling one of his assistants as I was going under the anesthetic.

I awoke in the most pleasant hospital setting I have ever experienced. It was a maternity hospital in the center of Bangkok but remarkably quiet and clean. My window faced an inner courtyard with high walls completely covered by the heavy roots and branches of flowering trees. I could see several women in the garden and four peacocks pecking around the grass and bushes, their tails in full flower most of the time.

Women with buckets and mops came to clean the room three or four times those next two days and an American my age with long blond hair was in the room across from me, due to give birth within hours. I could hear children and whole families visiting other patients. They must have brought food and games, because the sounds were those of a picnic.

Joe slept in a long chair beside the bed that night and bought me a gold bracelet set with small black star sapphires and rubies. The next day, the doctor sent us back to Vientiane with the cheerful prognosis that within a year we would have our first child and that we should send him a telegram when it happened. He was off by only four months, and we did send him the telegram.

Going Home

When we returned from the Bangkok hospital, the secretary of our project and her husband gave a party for a number of us soon to leave Vientiane. Despite our usual preoccupation with travel preparations and the accompanying feeling that we had halfway left already, that gathering crystalized for me the fact that Vientiane had nurtured close friendships. We sat on a wide window ledge eating meatballs and fresh salad and apple pie with a thin crust. Our hostess sat with us for a few minutes and we agreed on the things we would always remember about Vientiane. I still have her beef roulades recipe from that evening, and although I have never tried it, for a few seconds I think I can recall the peppery garlic taste.

Our last job was to find a container for taking the cats home. It had to be strong enough to keep them inside and to withstand hard bumps from the outside, airy enough to keep them comfortable, and small enough to put under our seats on the plane. After considering and rejecting cardboard cartons with air holes and slatted orange crates with splinters, we found the answer on the road outside the USAID compound.

A vendor was selling small household articles of rattan that he had made himself—fruit baskets, stools and tables, toy animals. Through an interpreter, we explained the purpose of our request and the specifications and general low rectangular shape required, drawing pictures in the dust where he squatted in front of his stall. For the next few days, we passed by the stall curiously, watching him work intently without once looking up, winding together golden strands of bamboo and turning small screws into hinges.

The finished product was a perfect combination of beauty and usefulness. The walls of the box were a grillwork of thin bamboo bars, anchored into a wooden floor. The lid, attached with hinges and of the same grillwork bamboo bars, was curved in a quarter circle so that the cats could press their heads against it comfortably when they stood up and stretched. The craftsman also pointed out through a demonstration that a curved lid prevented anyone from putting something on top of it. The lid was fastened by inserting and knotting a piece of wood through a rattan loop. There were no sharp edges or rough surfaces. Attached by a cord was a light blue flowered cloth ready to be placed over the lid if the outside world became too much for the cats to absorb. We found out from our interpreter that the cloth had been added by the craftsman's wife.

The box served its purpose. It made an inobtrusive package on the airplanes and in the hotels. It was not until the taxi ride home from the Pittsburgh airport that Sam finally pushed out one of the bars on the side. We seldom used it again as a cat carrier because it was not sturdy enough to put into the pet section of airplanes. But it serves well beside our fireplace as a box for storing logs, and has not lost any of its airy design, smooth surfaces, and pleasing shape.

When we first saw the finished box on the Vientiane roadside and expressed our delight, its maker smiled slightly and nodded his head, then frowned with embarrassment when we paid him more than the small amount he was asking. He hunkered down into his work position and began another project as we walked away. I glanced back several times to see whether he would watch us leave, but he never looked up.

. . .

Going
Back

. . .

The River

My first view of Vientiane again was twenty-two years later, from across the Mekong, sitting at a riverside restaurant in Thailand in the early evening. We had just said good-bye to our oldest daughter, who was volunteering for two months with a Thai development project fifty miles away.

The restaurant, billed as the best in town, was in a disheveled state. All its tables were piled high with dishes of half-eaten noodles, chicken bones, and crumpled pink napkins. Two giggly waitresses dragged their feet in duck walks across the plank floor, leaning over our shoulders and breathing in our ears as we looked at the menu; a singer whined in falsetto on the radio; and one stump-tailed brown cat wound in and out of the table legs. A few other diners came after us, including three young Americans with long legs, shorts, and gaunt, friendly faces and a middle-age Chinese couple who ate in silence. A group of eight or nine children hung over the rails from a jetty nearby, shouting at us in English and waving across the dark.

I looked to the river for some distraction, focusing on our ferry trip across it the next morning to Vientiane. The river was dark and gleaming, moving at a slow roll that suggested a depth surprising for the dry season. A rose-colored light beamed halfway across to us from a boat on the opposite shore, which, incredibly, had the silhouette of a large yacht. A slight rain dripped from the trees onto the water, combining with the steady chirping of insects. The fluorescent lights from the houses on the other shore glowed onto the water, outlining in blue-white a number of skiffs pulled up on the banks. The rest of Vientiane was black and invisible.

Back at our hotel, I wrote a letter to our daughter telling her not to stay any longer than prompted by her own interest and enthusiasm.

Openings

Our morning ride across the river to Vientiane was in the company of three Furies with unruly hair and gleaming smiles who had flown onto the running boards of our cyclo as we pulled into the ferry station, grabbed our bags, and lugged them to the dock. They spent the ten-minute ride on the tender haggling with us and among themselves as to how much we should pay them. We paid what we originally bargained for, which was evidently not satisfactory, since once we were on the Vientiane bank, they refused to carry the bags up the long flight of stairs to the station at the top.

The station crowd waiting for private cars or taxis or cyclos included street merchants as I remembered them, with flowered shirts and large straw baskets full of fruit and plain-wrapped goods, plus a new group—men in cotton and silk business suits with shiny briefcases and shoes, stepping into chauffeur-driven cars with darkened windows. We stepped into an American-variety car from the U.S. Embassy, a bright blue Oldsmobile with velvet seats, which took us to our room at the Souvanna Phouma Guest House, once the home of the former prime minister.

Our room had been his bedroom, we were told, in fact the room in which he died. The building was still being transformed from a private villa into a hotel, with staff sitting casually in the reception rooms and sleeping on the benches under the garden pavilions. One or two men at a time were hammering and digging, between long sessions of talking and smoking. A woman in heavy makeup picked at the bar piano, while another kept trying to show some photographs to a man in a dark suit.

Our room was old-style colonial with high ceilings and fans, two double beds, pink and white lace curtains, and a series of shuttered windows that opened out onto a balcony, a parched garden, and a view of the river. Blazing white fluorescent lights had been installed along all the balconies and across the entrance, so that at night, the former villa had a Las Vegas veneer.

It was difficult to tell how many of the other guests were overnighters like us, or there temporarily for lunch or dinner. But it was clear that their general purpose was business. They met in the lounge with secretaries, to whom they dictated from briefcases open on their laps, and they made many telephone calls from the one available instrument beside the reception desk. The frequency of their calls was due to the fact that most of the time the system cut them off in mid-conference. Some spoke Japanese, some Thai, a few German and English. Those who stayed overnight had all left for town in their dark-windowed cars by 9 A.M. and the only other time we saw signs of them was when we met two men in jogging shoes on the stairs at 7 A.M.

We lunched that first day at the villa of the American chargé d'affaires, whose long carpeted and tiled rooms and delicately cooked American food nurtured a relaxed conversation about Laos. The country was opening up to Thailand and Western capitalism and moving away from Vietnamese control—with the encouragement of the Soviets. Although worried about exploitation of its natural resources, especially from Thailand, the Lao seemed to be grabbing at offers. Women were starting to dress in bright silks and well-crafted shoes again, taking their jewelry out of storage. People who had been lounging on the streets for years since 1975 were now opening shops, painting buildings, and repairing. People were intently watching TV broadcast from Thailand, desiring the clothes and appliances and vehicles that were available so close across the river. When an Australian recently reported that Laos was a socialist economy, a Lao official retorted adamantly, "No, we're a *mixed* economy." At the last regional and national elections, some Party members were actually shifted downward at the lower levels of the bureaucracy.

Searching for Home

On the wall of the guest house dining room was a 1970 map of Vientiane—drawn by the Service Géographique—that clearly indicated the street where we used to live. A city map drawn for *Vientiane Guide* in 1988—a year before our visit—seemed to indicate the same road—coming from the monument, take two left turns off That Luang Road across a rice paddy. We set out on rented bicycles late one afternoon to find our former house.

The monument no longer had its look of finery, since the blue and white paint had long disappeared and the stone surface had reverted to an elephantine gray, with a faint pink glow from the setting sun. We rounded the plaza and turned right onto That Luang, joining clusters of cyclists, trucks, and cars returning home for dinner. We rode past our former colleague's high two-story house of the bewildering rooms, its garish outside now unremarkable, painted all white and hemmed in by identical neighbors.

In the heavy traffic, we kept our heads turned left, looking for that dirt road across a paddy that we imagined was now paved. The paddy was still there, about the same size, but the semipaved left turn across it took us to the drive gates of several large houses facing each other, which blocked further access. I thought I could see over to the left, through a clump of palm trees, the concrete latticing of the back wall of our house and maybe even the roofs of our former neighbors. But no city map indicated how to get through the new suburban labyrinth of short roads and houses that snaked around our old one.

We spent the next hour taking other left turns down red dirt roads, winding past children playing on bicycles, barking dogs, and people working in their gardens. Most of the houses we passed had features that looked familiar—white concrete surfaces, one story, cutout patterns in the walls and eaves, water towers in back—but none was quite right. We lost confidence in our memories—maybe That Luang was not even the right road. We tried the next one parallel to it, tried finding a back way, and ended up in a conclave of traditional Lao wooden houses on stilts where we politely declined an invitation to visit from a young woman sweeping the dirt path to her door.

Our last attempt was the same as our first, the road ending at several drive gates. We talked over one gate to the wife of the German ambassador, who explained that the paddy had been filled in years ago to provide for more house building and that now, because of inadequate drainage, their ground floors were flooded almost every rainy season.

We pedaled back to town in the growing darkness. My last glimpse of what must have been our house was the edge of a roof and the filigree of a white concrete wall almost completely hidden from the road by broad palm leaves.

Revisits

The former USAID compound had become a ghost town. The gate at one end of the main street was hanging wide open and crooked on partial hinges and the yellow lines marking the parking lanes were gone. There was concrete only intermittently on the roadway; the rest was reverting to gravel. The buildings were varieties of gray with a few strips of white paint, and all the windows were impenetrable, either boarded or tied across with plastic curtains. The only reminders of the former bustling motor pool were three dusty cars parked at odd angles in front of the one functioning building, which housed the Lao government offices. We saw only two staff members go out and in, both secretaries of the Lao official who summoned us there for an interview.

Our former office building was recognizable only because we remembered its position at the far end of the compound. Its two front entrances had been closed with black painted cement and the side entrance had no door at all. We got off our bicycles and looked down the long narrow hall with a few pieces of familiar tile left and saw the closed door on the right that had been our office entry. I remembered walking down that hall my first day of work and being introduced to the USAID director, who looked fresh and military in an unwrinkled seersucker suit.

The open doorway at the other end of the hall let in the late-afternoon sun. Through its rays stepped a black chicken, who paused, lifted one foot, and then walked out again around the corner. As we turned to go, a man on a motorcycle with a small girl riding behind stopped and asked us in English what we were looking for. He did not return our smiles and asked the same question two more times as we biked away.

■ ■ ■

The Lan Xang hotel was full—tourists from Thailand and visiting
delegations from thirteen countries, a longtime employee told us.
He mentioned several times the names of two newsmen, one
American and one Australian, who often stayed at the hotel and
knew him well. He took us through the glass doors of the large
reception room where we had attended the Rotary Club affair. It
was dusty but looked in use and had been expanded into a second room for small banquets. Our guide took us around the
lobby with its new shops selling Lao handicrafts at one-third
more than the same articles sold for on the street.

We could not identify for certain the USAID house we had
stayed in our first two weeks in 1967. It was one of three almost
identical ones standing in a row outside the compound walls. All
had decayed in equal measure, with boards sagging on the side
walls, peeling strips of light green paint, boarded-over windows,
and a few pieces of splintered latticing at the base of each front
porch. On the roof of the one on the left—which may have been
ours—a TV aerial bent over the roof.

We pedaled around the curve in the road, still red dust,
where the carpenter had made the rattan basket for transporting
our cats. Behind a building that still had its Service Géographique
sign, we searched in vain among parked flatbed trucks for the
grass tennis court once in constant use.

■ ■ ■

I shopped for books and gifts on the two shopping streets of
Vientiane. A bookstore that may have been there twenty-two
years ago was clerked by two sullen women, one of whom lay
stretched out on a counter for part of the time. Almost all the
books were in Russian—texts, children's books, handbooks, biographies, magazines, novels—except for one section in Vietnamese and several in English, including a translation of a Party
history and a collection of Lao government statistics.

Against a back wall beside larger-than-life-size posters of the

Lao Party leaders was a case displaying notepaper with crude ink drawings of jungles and huts, and one peculiar set of Czarist soldiers in high hats and feathers tilted against a mélange of animals and figures in Russian peasant costume. A shop next door, which sold some of the same books and had much friendlier clerks, featured Lao handicrafts—heavy woven cotton bags and long cloths of traditional patterns and some of brighter colors and bolder patterns to accommodate modern tastes.

Later, I passed the Indian shop where we had bought our living room woolen rugs with the floral patterns arranged like spokes of a wheel. Instead of our salesman—an Indian with a stately, portly carriage and white hair—the shop was watched by a teenage boy who sat sideways to the street with his feet upon a display case. He moved only his face in my direction as I paused at the door.

I was almost the only customer on the streets, but the plentiful amount of goods on all the shelves indicated that more were expected. One moment of frenzied buying occurred when a group of four Russian women clustered around the one display case of a silver shop. This place was run by a Vietnamese woman who directed three Lao boys lined up across the back wall in the design and production of silver jewelry of great refinement. The Russian women leaned on the glass, talking with tension and heat, pulling each other's bare arms, and stabbing their fingers on the glass at their choices. Their harried looks and impatient motions seemed odd in the heat and quiet of the street.

Pictures and Words

On the front of every Lao government publication is the official seal, invented in 1975 at the emergence of the Lao Peoples Democratic Republic. Across the seal, images and words jostle each other with exuberance and no indication of priorities. Its general shape is a crescent, formed by two stalks of rice with long curling leaves, ready to be harvested. These stalks curve upward, almost meeting at the top. Intertwined at their base are three pieces of drapery with words in Lao. The one to the left reads, *Peace, Independence;* at the center, *Lao Peoples Democratic Republic;* and to the right, *Unity, Socialism.* At the top, lodged between the tips of the rice stalks, is the Communist star suspended above a hammer and sickle.

Crowded below this heavy skyline is a countryside of trees, a rice paddy, a paved road, a derrick piling up mounds of earth, and a dam holding back a wide river. The top half of a large cogged wheel emerges in the foreground, while in the background, beyond the walls of the dam, appears the head of a large reindeer conversing with a duck who is gesticulating with outstretched wings.

At least that is what I first saw, until informed that the conversing animals were really vaguely drawn electrical power lines.

Laos was traditionally called The Land of the Million Elephants. Its official seal was a royal parasol under which a three-headed elephant looked east, south, and west. Vientiane, a Lao explained to us, means City of Sandalwood. *Vien* signifies not only *city* but also *place of the royal house. Tiane,* sandalwood, is a perfume tree common in India and plentiful on the outskirts of Vientiane. It is burned only as a Buddhist offering, especially at funerals.

A Chinese-Thai friend gave us an alternative interpretation of Vientiane—City of the Moon.

Talking with Lao

A Lao employee at the U.S. Embassy told us the story of the young woman who had been a translator for our project in 1967, whom I last remembered serenely bending over her firstborn, week-old son. In 1975, her husband was sent to a reeducation camp, where he was confined for eight years. She took care of their four sons and worked for the United Nations. It was a sad time when her husband was released, because he was angry and suspicious that she had a foreign boyfriend, and the two argued continually. After working briefly for the Lao government, he and their two older sons crossed the river one day and eventually emigrated to California. Two years later, she left with the two younger boys, for Paris and Geneva.

The Lao official who talked with us in his dark, airless office with too much space spoke with me first on a hot street corner where we met by chance. A delicate man in his late sixties with whitewashed-looking skin, he wore completely unwrinkled tan cotton pants, a shirt with a modified Chinese collar, and pointed leather shoes. His hand was cold when I shook it. He asked me in formal French whether I was enjoying my visit. I answered that I liked Vientiane and remembered with pleasure our stay in 1967. He looked slightly displeased for a moment, then nodded.

I later interpreted this reaction as his being not particularly happy to hear that Vientiane 1967 was enjoyable under the old Royal Lao Government, since at that time he was a Pathet Lao official hiding in a cave with his family in Sam Neua province to escape from American and RLG bombing. Later in his office, his answers to questions about present government policy and history were deliberate, impersonal, and courteous, with no surprises. He prolonged the session with chain-smoking and pouring many cups of tea.

The deserted atmosphere of his office and desk—with a few books and papers piled neatly on either side of a large blotter—and our suspicion that he was there for our benefit only were replicated in the other government office I visited. The old building, formerly housing the French provincial administration, seemed practically uninhabited, with three men and two women leaning against the entranceway in relaxed conversation. A secretary came down a long hall, his shoes clicking on the tile floor, and ushered me into a room with only an empty desk, where two restless Germans and a Lao were already seated in straight-backed spindle chairs. The secretary gave me his chair and walked awkwardly back and forth among us, apologizing for the wait.

My most frequent Lao contacts were with the staff at our guest house, where I needed to order breakfast and ask for more toilet paper and towels. Our breakfast waiter never spoke, which kept us continually in the dark about his knowledge of English. He was invariably deferent and gentle, and a little downcast, belying his perky black bow tie. He brought me ham and two fried eggs when I pointed to a plate not yet cleared to indicate I needed something on which to put my toast. He brought a large bottled water when I asked for tea, and when Joe asked for a soft-boiled egg by drawing a picture of one in an eggcup, he got more ham and two fried eggs.

These misunderstandings were distressing to all three of us, because we were all trying hard to be accommodating. I searched for another level by thanking him in English and then asking him what the Lao word was for *thank you*. I tried out *Sop chai* and repeated it several times. He left and then immediately returned with a bottle of orange juice and a fork and then looked sad when I shook my head. I concluded that getting into such complexities was only deepening everyone's frustration.

Several of the young girls on the staff, on the other hand, were casual, even familiar in their manner. When one shook her head and started to walk away as I was asking for more toilet paper, I figured that, unlike our waiter, she had no patience for requests in English. I took her by the arm and led her to a window, pointing to some paper rolls leaning against the glass. Another time, on the day of our departure, I walked into our room as two maids were cleaning it and was startled to see one sitting on the bed while another slowly turned in front of the mirror, modeling her skirt. They did not change positions or stop their conversation after I entered.

The staff seemed to be composed of rustics, pleased to be in a former prime minister's villa and untrained in professional behavior. Their supervisors alleviated the guests' frustrations by devoting themselves to getting long-distance phone calls through, replacing light bulbs, and delivering towels in person.

Talking with Russians

During my early-morning walks along the road across from our guest house, I passed a cluster of villas described to us as the Russian compound. At one house in particular, there were always a woman and little girl with schoolbag and lunch box waiting at the foot of a long gravel driveway. They both looked old-fashioned in some way, like a 1940s advertisement in the Norman Rockwell style, maybe because of the girl's blond braids and large hair ribbon and the woman's plain cotton dress—what used to be called a housedress.

I strode past self-consciously in my heavy jogging shoes and said good morning. The woman politely looked away as I first appeared, then nodded in a return greeting. The little girl only looked. When I returned by the same route, they were gone. I stared eagerly through the iron railings at the yard and house inside, hoping to see something distinctively Russian. I caught glimpses of some plastic toys and a dark blue sedan.

The day before we left Vientiane, we spent three hours at the Soviet Embassy talking with two officials, one of whom served as interpreter. The latter, who met us at the door, was in his thirties, pale and handsome, with light eyes and hair, finely cut features, and an intense, whimsical manner. His English was only slightly accented, almost always correct, and imaginative. He left us sitting at a low round table covered with teapot and cups, a coffeepot, biscuits, potato sticks, bottles of soda, and a bowl of Russian chocolates wrapped in foil and turquoise paper depicting a mother bear and three cubs playing on a fallen tree. The interpreter later offered me some of the chocolates and when I hesitated, he said, "If you are worried about your figure, don't—it's not dangerous."

He returned with a senior colleague, large and rosy, dressed in a white short-sleeved shirt without a tie. His facial expressions were modest and sardonic by turn and his gestures large and curved to accommodate the heavy weight and shape of his shoulders and arms. His language—in English translation—seemed more careful and less subtle than his colleague's, delivered after a slight frown and pause. When we later discovered we could all speak directly in French, he requested, nevertheless, that we return to Russian and English because the translations gave him time to think.

Our three hours together were interrupted only once, by two women who came in to refill the tea and coffee pots. One was composed, with glasses, and the other was younger—although I only saw her peripherally—leaving behind her an impression of blondness, height, and grace.

The conversation flowed and eddied between Joe's questions and our host's answers, kept in motion by the quick understanding of the interpreter. The subjects were Laos and Indochina, which our host knew well because he had served in the Soviet Embassy in Hanoi for eleven years before coming to Laos in 1988. He pressed his general message: that for Laos, the Indochina scene was not one of confrontation and power politics, as the questions put to him implied, but, rather, a new era of economic cooperation; that Laos was building a socialist economy on a new, more democratic model under pragmatic, nondogmatic leadership.

He paused the longest, in the final hour, over his own three questions: How does Laos 1967 compare to Laos today? Does the U.S. government take seriously its decertification of Laos for aid because of Laotian opium production? How do Americans regard the recent changes in economic policy in Laos? He took notes in a plain cloth-covered notebook, with the kind of thick pearly fountain pen that I remember seeing forty-five years ago on my father's desk.

The interpreter was a virtuoso. He did not seem to miss the subtleties of such phrases in English as *I would like to make an observation if I may* or *I agree with you for the most part but differ in interpretation of Vietnam's motives.* When he rendered these into Russian, his facial expressions, gestures, and voice changes strongly suggested dependent clauses and qualifiers and courteous interjections. When he listened, he accompanied the English speaker with "m-hmm, m-hmm" and the Russian with "da-da-da." His translations of his colleague's responses tended to the formal and abstract. He twice spoke of the "perfection" of a system when he meant "development," and once he broke into a French root when he said "I would devine . . ." rather than "I would guess."

We told them of our recent visit to Odessa and the eagerness with which people talked to us. I told them of hearing a haunting song about taking care of the earth that was performed there by a high school chorus. Our host nodded solemnly and said, "The world is small and precious."

At 8 P.M., we stood up at the table with its plates emptied and its tea drunk and walked outside on the embassy grounds in the fading light. A large group of children and adults were playing volleyball, shouting and diving expertly for each shot.

Early Morning

The neighborhood across from our guest house combined suburban and rural Vientiane. Our early-morning walks along its dirt roads took us past men and women with shoulder bags and the occasional briefcase, moving intently toward us and the highway to town. Groups of cows herded by children, and chickens and dogs, and people with rolled-up pant legs crossed back and forth over the road and into the fields and paddies. Walking and weaving along on bicycles in the same direction as we, were groups of schoolchildren in white shirts and dark pants and skirts. Many rode double on their shiny bicycles, glancing back and smiling as they passed us, a few shouting *"So bai dee"* (Hello) and then giggling. The animals roamed with impunity across the front yards of Lao huts and cement villas alike.

We started off early to catch the cool air and red dirt road when it was still packed from the rain the night before. Cows, some black, some red, some spotted, stood together in bright green fields, resting their jaws on each other's backs or into the high grass, resembling the stark asymmetrical forms and flat colors of Japanese woodcuts. Rainbow roosters high stepped between the stilts of wooden houses and in and out of fences and yards, glaring disdainfully. New chicks, some of them looking more like quail, tumbled after their parents.

A few houses had elegant goats with Siamese cat markings. They must have been considered valuable, since the adults were chained, while their kids bounced alongside. The ducks were either all brown or black-and-white spotted, with dark pink skin around their bills. They spent that time of the morning cleaning themselves in the mud puddles. Most of the dogs, who greeted each other and then went off on rounds, were a uniform tan, some part German shepherd, some a longer-haired sheep dog mix. The ones in their own yards barked at us and we always crossed to the other side of the road when passing one shepherd bitch who was a nervous nursing mother.

We probably did seem odd and out of rhythm with the usual movement on the road, striding along in forced march in our jogging shoes, swinging our arms. Those who had not gone to town walked slowly and softly, mostly in sandals and slightly duckfooted. The women were wrapped in long skirts, sweeping front cement porches with rush brooms and carrying large water jars. At one wooden hut with a long tin roof, the front yard was almost all dirt except for vestiges of a cement drive. A woman was hoeing furrows between the flat cement blocks while a child of two or three, in only a shirt, followed her and scraped at the mud with a stick.

A few of the villas were painted a color other than white and had gardens of cactus plants, placed together for their contrasts in size and shape, and small circles of purely decorative grass ringed with white stones. All houses, whether wooden or cement, had an airy look, with openings of slats or filigreed concrete, which caught the sunlight and must have thrown ornate shadows into the rooms beneath.

On our last morning, one girl of about seven, with schoolbooks on her back and dressed in white blouse, long skirt, and sandals, spun around in the road ahead and ran back straight at me. She was calling in a piercing nasal voice, her arms and sandals flapping. Her anxiety was infectious, and for a moment I thought I was under attack for committing some indiscretion. But it became obvious she was aiming for an older girl behind me as she flew past like a dark bird.

Going Out

Our last day in Vientiane was two days before our twenty-fifth wedding anniversary. We went to the silver shop where I had seen the Russian women buying jewelry with great animation, and I chose two silver necklaces. The longer one is twisted strands of silver, like a rope, and the other is made of flat slivers encrusted in slanted patterns that glint like jewels. For a few minutes, we watched the three Lao boys in the back of the shop burning similarly delicate pieces out of black hunks of pure silver. The severe Vietnamese patroness directed them while greeting customers with a steely smile.

We left for Bangkok on a small propeller plane with parts marked with Russian labels. The Bangkok airport was humming and jostling and orderly. The Thai English-language newspaper headlines heralded a conference of regional leaders being held that week, called by the Thai prime minister "to turn war-ravaged Indochina into a marketplace." Headlines elaborated on this theme: TALKS ON THAI-JAPAN TRADE IMBALANCE AWAIT TAKESHITA; KHMER FACTIONS INSIST THAT VIETNAMESE TROOP WITHDRAWAL MUST BE MONITORED BY THE UNITED NATIONS; CHATICHAI: THERE MUST BE ONE SOUTHEAST ASIA; VIETNAM ASKS THAILAND TO ACT AS REGIONAL COORDINATOR.

Attending the conference were the Vietnamese Deputy Prime Minister and Foreign Minister, the Vietnamese Commissioner of Social Sciences, the Lao Ambassador to Thailand, the Lao Commerce and Economics Minister, the North Korean Deputy Prime Minister, the chairman of the Board of Trade for Thailand, Thai editors, the general manager of the Banque Française du Commerce Extérieur, the president of the U.S. Chamber of Commerce, and the Australian editor of the *Asian Wall Street Journal*.

We flew from Bangkok to Hong Kong amidst a tremendous din of young Asians expensively dressed and carrying large shopping bags overflowing with packages. They held in their laps and under their arms and feet the packages that could not be stuffed in the overhead racks or under the seats, and joked and shouted and pushed at each other in celebration.